# FOSS Correlation

## Earth Science

**Earth Materials Module**
(Earth materials; crystal geology; mineral rock properties)
12, 13, 14, 15, 16, 17, 18, 19, 20, 33, 34, 35, 36, 46, 47, 51, 52, 53

**Water Module**
(Properties and states; water cycle; condensation; evaporation; surface tension)
21, 22, 23, 24, 25, 26, 27, 28, 29, 30, 31, 32, 37, 43

## Life Science

**Structures of Life Module**
(Fruit; seeds; changes and properties of growth; structure and behavior of animals; habitats and populations)
41, 42, 43, 44, 45, 46, 47, 48, 49, 50, 51, 52, 53, 54, 55, 56, 57, 58, 66

**Human Body Module**
(Human skeleton; muscle structure and function; response and reaction time)
59, 60, 61, 62, 63, 64, 65, 82

## Physical Science

**Magnetism and Electricity Module**
(Magnets; electromagnets; attraction and repulsion; force; circuits; conductors and insulators)
67, 75, 76, 77, 78, 79, 80

**Physics of Sound Module**
(Sound sources and receivers; vibration; travel; pitch)
89, 90, 91, 92, 93, 94, 95, 96

## Scientific Reasoning

**Measurement Module**
(Tools for measurement: linear, volume, temperature, weight and mass)
22, 23, 24, 25, 26, 27, 31, 32, 33, 34, 35, 36, 39, 56, 57, 59, 68, 69, 70, 72, 73, 74

Name _____  Date _____

# Types of Projects

## A Collection Using Classifying

In a collection, you place items into groups according to their similar properties. The items should be science objects that you have collected. Your collection should not include stamps or coins or things that other people have collected. You should decide carefully on the categories, or groups, in which you will place the items. You should try to have several objects in each category. You should be able to explain how you grouped the objects when you present your project to the judges. For example, you might group rocks according to their color, their sparkle, or their source.

Each item on display should have a name or description. Your project should include the collection, a project notebook, and a posterboard display giving this information:

**TITLE** of the collection
**INFORMATION** about the collection
**CLASSIFICATION SCHEME** of the collected items

**Examples of collections**
feathers; eggshells; bird nests; seeds from grasses; pieces of bark; leaves; fossils; empty insect nests

## An Exhibit That Gives Information

An exhibit can be a model, a display, or a demonstration, with a report. The report part of this project is an essay, with pictures, that gives information about your exhibit. Make the exhibit and write the report yourself. Use several sources for the information in your exhibit. Your report should be clear and factual. Be able to explain your exhibit to the judges.

Your project should include the exhibit, a project notebook, and a posterboard display giving this information:

**TITLE** of the exhibit
**WRITTEN INFORMATION** about the exhibit (may include diagrams)
**EXPLANATION** of what the exhibit shows
**REFERENCES** (books, articles, Internet sites, or resource people used)

**Examples of exhibits**
**Demonstration:** You could demonstrate how light reflects off different things. You might set up mirrors and show how a beam of light from a flashlight bounces from one mirror to the next. Your report should explain that light travels in straight lines.
**Model:** You could make a cutaway model of the Earth out of clay. Labels could show the layers of the Earth, and your report could give information about each level.
**Display:** You could make a display about birds, showing pictures of different kinds of birds. Your report could tell where the birds live, what they eat, and some interesting habits of the birds.

Name _____  Date _____

# Types of Projects, page 2

**An Experiment That Answers a Question**

An experiment tries to answer a question. Good experiment questions are about things you think might be true. What you think is true is called your "hypothesis." Then, design an experiment or test that will show if your hypothesis is correct. Your experiment procedure should use the Scientific Method. Show samples, photos, or other proof that you really did the experiment. Show your "Conclusion" in charts or graphs. Read books to get more information about your topic. Use your own ideas and your own words. Be able to explain your experiment to the judges.

Your project should include the experiment equipment and proof, a project notebook, and a posterboard display giving this information:

**TITLE** of the experiment
**PROBLEM:** What question are you trying to answer?
**HYPOTHESIS:** What do you think the answer to your question is?
**EXPERIMENTATION:** What materials did you use to carry out the experiment? What did you do in your investigation?
**OBSERVATION:** What did you observe during the experiment? Take notes.
**CONCLUSION:** What happened in the experiment? What is the answer to the question in your "Problem"? How do you explain your results? (Use tables of data or graphs.)
**COMPARISON:** Does your conclusion agree with your hypothesis? If so, you have shown that your hypothesis was correct.
**PRESENTATION:** Prepare a presentation or report to share your findings.
**RESOURCES:** Include a list of resources used. You need to give credit to books or people that helped you with your work.

**Examples of experiments**

Do ants like diet soda? Does sound travel at the same speed through all objects? Does warm water freeze faster than cold water?

Name _____   Date _____

# Science Fair Checklist

The science fair at your school is a good place to show your science skills and knowledge. You need to think about your project carefully so that it will show your best work. Use the Scientific Method to help you to organize your project. Here are some other things to consider:

**PROJECT TITLE** _____

| Working Plan | Date Due | Date Completed | Teacher Initials |
|---|---|---|---|
| 1. Select topic | | | |
| 2. Explore resources | | | |
| 3. Start notebook | | | |
| 4. Form hypothesis | | | |
| 5. Find materials | | | |
| 6. Investigate | | | |
| 7. Prepare results | | | |
| 8. Prepare summary | | | |
| 9. Plan your display | | | |
| 10. Construct your display | | | |
| 11. Complete notebook | | | |
| 12. Prepare for judging | | | |

Write a brief paragraph describing the hypothesis, materials, and procedures you will include in your exhibit. Be sure to plan your project carefully. Get all the materials and resources you need beforehand. A good presentation should have plenty of visual aids, so use pictures, charts, and other things to make your project easier to understand.

Be sure to follow all the rules for your school science fair. Also, be prepared for the judging part. The judges will want to see a clear and thorough presentation of your data and resources. They will also want to see that you understand your project and can tell them about it clearly and thoroughly. Good luck!

Name _____  Date _____

# The Scientific Method

Did you know you think and act like a scientist? You can prove it by following these steps when you have a problem. These steps are called the Scientific Method.

**1. PROBLEM:** Identify a problem or question to investigate.
_____
_____

**2. HYPOTHESIS:** Tell what you think will be the result of your investigation or activity.
_____
_____

**3. EXPERIMENTATION:** Perform the investigation or activity.
_____

**4. OBSERVATION:** Make observations, and take notes about what you observe.
_____
_____
_____

**5. CONCLUSION:** Draw conclusions from what you have observed.
_____
_____
_____

**6. COMPARISON:** Does your conclusion agree with your hypothesis? If so, you have shown that your hypothesis was correct. If not, do not go back and change your hypothesis. Write a revised hypothesis that tells what you discovered.
_____

**7. PRESENTATION:** Prepare a presentation or report to share your findings.

**8. RESOURCES:** Include a list of resources used. You need to give credit to people or books you used to help you with your work.
_____
_____

Name _____   Date _____

# Your Science Fair Project

You have just picked a topic that you want to know more about. Use this sheet to record information about your project.

Project topic _____

Questions I have about my topic _____
_____
_____

Materials I will need for my project _____
_____

How I will set up my project _____
_____
_____

Draw a sketch to show how your finished project will look.

```
┌──────────────────────────────────────────────────────┐
│                                                      │
│                                                      │
│                                                      │
│                                                      │
│                                                      │
│                                                      │
└──────────────────────────────────────────────────────┘
```

Observations I made during my project _____
_____
_____

What I discovered about my topic _____
_____
_____

Name _____  Date _____

# Science Fair Notebook

The science fair notebook helps you to organize all your information about your project. Work hard to prepare a neat, carefully arranged notebook.

In your notebook, include as many of these parts as possible:

## TITLE PAGE
This should include the title of the project, the type of project, the student's name, the teacher's name, and the date of the science fair.

## TABLE OF CONTENTS
This is a listing of the parts inside the notebook and their page numbers.

## HYPOTHESIS
If you are doing an experiment, state the hypothesis and include an explanation of why you chose to test this hypothesis.

## MATERIALS
This page contains a detailed listing of all materials used in the project. Be as specific as possible.

## RESEARCH
This section should include all the information you collected to prepare the project. Include a summary for each source listed in the Resources section.

## EXPERIMENTATION
If you are doing an experiment, include all the steps taken in testing your hypothesis. The information should be clear and thorough. Each step should include all observations, notes, and supporting graphs, charts, drawings, or photos.

## CONCLUSION
In this section, you should analyze the notes collected during the experiment. Then, you should state whether the results support the hypothesis.

## RESOURCES USED
List all the books, magazines, newspapers, or interviews that you summarized in the Research section.

Neatly arrange all your parts in a binder or folder. You might also include the title of your project on the cover.

Name _____   Date _____

# Presenting the Project

An important part of the science project is the presentation. You must display your project so others can understand your work. Your display should be neatly done and sturdy enough to last through the science fair. Your display should be designed so the materials and equipment are not dangerous.

Be sure that you know the rules of your school science fair. You will be assigned an amount of space for your project, often 2 to 4 feet of table space. Check to see if your school will allow a project to use electricity or glass containers.

Your display can be made of 2 to 4 panels of a sturdy material such as cardboard, pegboard, or wood. The panels should be able to stand and support themselves after being fastened together with tape or hinges.

All titles should be done neatly and be self-explanatory. The title of the project should be placed across the top of the middle panel. Subtitles should follow the Scientific Method, and include such headings as problem, hypothesis, experiment, methods, results, and conclusion.

Make sure your charts and graphs are neatly done. Color graphs are recommended. Photographs, computer graphics, and drawings should be neatly arranged on the display. Label all the materials on display.

Study the display below for ideas.

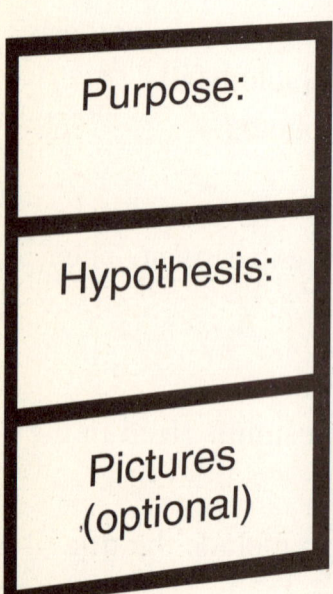
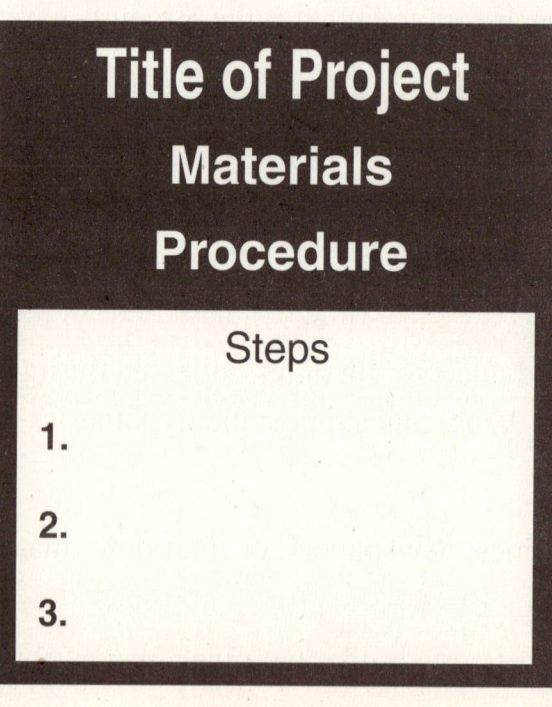
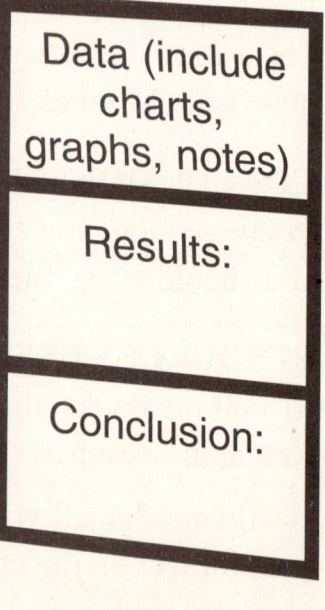

Equipment                                    Materials

Name _____  Date _____

# Earth Science Project

A science fair project can help you to understand the world around you better. Choose a topic that interests you. Then, use the Scientific Method to develop your project. Here's an example:

1. **PROBLEM:** How does the Earth's rotation cause day and night?

2. **HYPOTHESIS:** A demonstration with a flashlight and a globe turning can show how the Earth's rotation causes day and night.

3. **EXPERIMENTATION:** Do a demonstration. Find your state on the globe. Darken the room, and then shine a flashlight at the globe. Slowly turn the globe around once.

4. **OBSERVATION:** Observe when daylight begins in your state and when night begins.

5. **CONCLUSION:** When the light first shines on your state is when daylight begins. When the light is no longer shining on your state is when night begins.

6. **COMPARISON:** The conclusion agrees with the hypothesis.

7. **PRESENTATION:** Present this demonstration to the judges. Hold the flashlight 2 feet from the globe. Move the globe to give the experience of both day and night. Include diagrams and information about the rotation of the Earth on your display. You might want to mention the longest and shortest days of the year.

8. **RESOURCES:** Tell who helped you get the flashlight and the globe. Include any books, magazines, or Internet sites that you used to help you write your report.

1. What are some inventions scientists have created for space travel? One is the rechargeable battery. Do research on materials made for space missions. Then, present a collection of these items that we now use every day.
2. What is the new type of star discovered in 1998? It is called a magnetar. Where is it located? Read news magazines and science magazines to find out about it. Then, do a display and report on it.
3. What is the inside of the Sun like? Do research and make a model of the Sun.

Name _____  Date _____

# How Hard Is a Rock?

Rocks can be used in many ways. You decide how a rock can be used by studying its properties. Some rocks are hard, and some are soft. Some are strong, and some break easily. Strong rocks wear away slowly.

A rock is often a mineral. One way minerals can be identified is by their hardness. Look at the table. It rates ten kinds of minerals by this property. It is known as Mohs' Hardness Scale.

## MOHS' HARDNESS SCALE

| Mineral | Hardness Rating |
|---|---|
| talc | 1 |
| gypsum | 2 |
| calcite | 3 |
| fluorite | 4 |
| apatite | 5 |
| orthoclase | 6 |
| quartz | 7 |
| topaz | 8 |
| corundum | 9 |
| diamond | 10 |

| Object | Hardness Rating |
|---|---|
| fingernail | 2.5 |
| penny | 3 |
| nail | 5 |
| steel file | 6.5 |

How hard is a rock? You can check. Some soft rocks can be scratched with a fingernail.

**MATERIALS**

steel nail 5–6 cm long
masking tape for 4 labels
safety goggles
4 different kinds of rocks
penny
pen
paper

Name _____ Date _____

# How Hard Is a Rock?, page 2

**PROCEDURE**

1. Put masking tape on each rock. Label the rocks **1**, **2**, **3**, and **4**.
2. Since it is possible for small chips to fly when scratching rocks with a nail, wear the safety goggles.
3. Try to scratch each rock.
4. Record what happens on the chart. Put an **X** in the chart if the rock was scratched.

| Rock | Fingernail | Penny | Nail |
|---|---|---|---|
| 1 | | | |
| 2 | | | |
| 3 | | | |
| 4 | | | |

**DRAWING CONCLUSIONS**

1. How many rocks could you scratch with your fingernail?
2. How many could you scratch with a penny?
3. How many could you scratch with a nail?
4. Which rock is hardest? How do you know?
5. Which rock is softest? How do you know?

**MORE IDEAS**

1. Include the four rocks and some of the minerals in the Mohs' Hardness Scale in your display.
2. Include the Mohs' Hardness Scale and your chart in your display.
3. Show the judges how the various objects can scratch the rocks or minerals.

Name _____ Date _____

# How Are Rocks Broken Down?

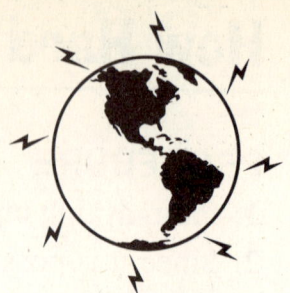

Rocks change and break. Breaking of rocks into pieces is called weathering. One way is when rainwater and carbon dioxide gas mix in the air. The water falls to the ground and goes into cracks. The rainwater makes the rocks break. Try this experiment to see how rocks are broken down.

### MATERIALS

| | | |
|---|---|---|
| 3 small jars | limestone rocks | water |
| vinegar | drinking straw | |
| 3 labels | crayon or pen | |

## PROCEDURE

1. Fill 2 jars half full of water. Label 1 jar **Water**.
2. Blow through the straw into the second jar of water. The air you blow out contains carbon dioxide gas. Label this jar **Carbon Dioxide**.
3. Fill the third jar half full of vinegar. Label this jar **Vinegar**.
4. Put some limestone rocks in each jar. Keep 1 rock set aside.
5. Let the rocks sit in the jars overnight. Record your observations the next day.
6. Fill in the chart with your observations.

| Jar | Changes in Rocks |
|---|---|
| Water | |
| Carbon Dioxide | |
| Vinegar | |

## DRAWING CONCLUSIONS

1. What changes did you see in the rocks?
2. How did the vinegar, the carbon dioxide, and the water change the rocks? Which of these caused the most weathering of the rocks?

**MORE IDEAS**

1. Include your setup and chart in your display.
2. Do research to learn what forces in nature cause weathering of rocks.
3. Which famous landforms are the result of weathering? Include pictures in your display.

Name _____  Date _____

# How Does a Volcano Erupt?

What does a volcano look like when it erupts? You can make a model of the top part of a volcano. This is the part that is above the Earth's surface.

### MATERIALS

| | | |
|---|---|---|
| wide pen | scissors | cone-shaped paper cup |
| paper | vinegar | petroleum jelly |
| plaster mix | water | baking soda |
| mixing pan | | |

## PROCEDURE

1. Mix the plaster with water in a mixing pan.
2. Pour the plaster into the cone-shaped cup.
3. Before the plaster hardens, turn the cup over and place it on a piece of paper.
4. Cut off the top part of the cone.
5. Coat the pen with petroleum jelly. Push it into the plaster to make a crater. Keep it there until the plaster begins to harden.
6. When the plaster is hard, peel off the paper cup. Paint or color the plaster cone if you like.
7. Pour baking soda into the crater. Add 2 or 3 drops of vinegar. Watch your model volcano erupt.

**MORE IDEAS**

1. Draw a diagram of a volcano. Show the parts above and below the Earth's surface. Include the diagram on your display.
2. Do research on some famous volcanoes. Include the information in your notebook.

Name _____  Date _____

# What Does Erosion Do?

Erosion is the breaking down and carrying away of soil and rocks. In this activity, you will see how erosion works.

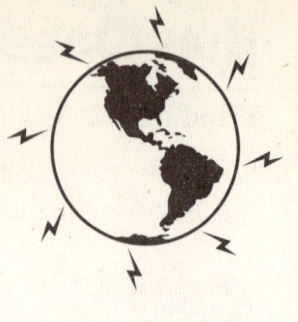

**MATERIALS**

large pan   water
sand        straw

## PROCEDURE

1. Put sand into the pan. Add water to make the sand wet. Shape the wet sand into landforms, such as mountains, plains, and plateaus. Put some dry sand on top of the landforms.
2. Pour water on the landforms. Pour a little bit of water slowly. Then, pour a lot of water quickly. Watch what happens.
3. Use the straw to blow against the landforms to model wind. Blow at different speeds and from different directions. Watch what happens.

## DRAWING CONCLUSIONS

1. What happened when water was added to the different landforms?
2. How did the wind affect the landforms?
3. Did the wind act in the same way on the wet sand and on the dry sand? Explain.

## MORE IDEAS

1. Include your setup in your display.
2. Do research to learn what forces in nature cause erosion.
3. Which famous landforms are the result of erosion? Include pictures in your display.

www.svschoolsupply.com
© Steck-Vaughn Company

Unit 1: Earth Science
Science Projects 3–4, SV 6910-8

Name _____ Date _____

# How Can Erosion Be Slowed?

Erosion is the breaking down and carrying away of soil and rocks. People can slow down erosion. Try this experiment to see one way.

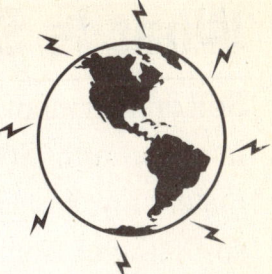

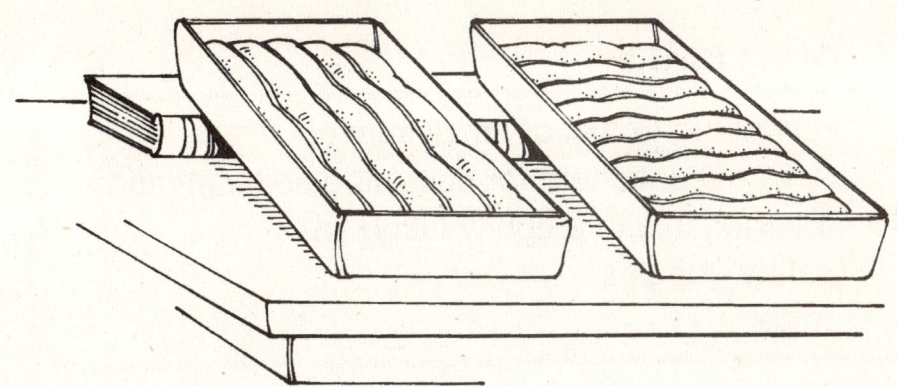

### MATERIALS

sprinkling can   2 large rectangular cake pans
2 books          sandy soil, 4 liters
water

## PROCEDURE

1. Pour some soil into each cake pan, and spread it evenly.
2. Make furrows, or grooves, across the length of one pan.
3. Make furrows across the width of the other pan.
4. Raise one end of each pan by leaning it against a book. Predict which field will erode faster.
5. Use a sprinkling can to pour water over the raised end of each field.

## DRAWING CONCLUSIONS

1. What do you see happening?
2. Draw a circle around the field that eroded faster. Was your prediction correct?

**MORE IDEAS**

1. Include your setup with your display.
2. Tell the judges your prediction. Then, do the experiment for the judges.
3. Do research to learn how farmers slow down erosion in their fields.

Name _____ Date _____

# What Is Soil Made Of?

Soil is the granular material that forms the top layer of much of the land on Earth. Soil is composed of ground-up rock, minerals, organic material, water, and air. In this project, you will investigate different soil samples from around your home to find out what they are made of.

**MATERIALS**

gardening trowel or small shovel
several containers for collecting soil samples
1 large jar with a tightly fitting lid
safety goggles
water

## PROCEDURE

1. Collect a small amount of soil from three areas near your home. Choose a variety of areas so that you get different kinds of soil samples. Place each soil sample in its own labeled container.
2. Fill the jar about one quarter full of one of the soil samples.
3. Add water until the jar is almost full, and put the lid on securely.
4. Shake the jar vigorously. CAUTION: Wear safety goggles for this step.
5. Wait for the soil to settle. The different materials your sample contains should settle out in layers.
6. Repeat Steps 2 through 5 with your other soil samples.
CAUTION: Wash your hands thoroughly when you finish handling the soil.

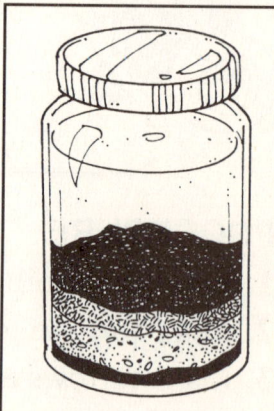

Wait for the soil to settle in layers.

## DRAWING CONCLUSIONS

1. Were the layers different depending on where you got your soil?
2. Did one seem more sandy?
3. Did any contain more humus (organic materials)?

## MORE IDEAS

1. Include your setup and soil samples in your display.
2. Select soil samples from an area that has many plants and an area that does not have many plants. Test the soil samples. What is in the soil where plants grow compared with the soil where plants do not grow? Plant some seeds (such as peas or beans) in each type of soil and see which is best for growing seeds.

www.svschoolsupply.com
© Steck-Vaughn Company

Unit 1: Earth Science
Science Projects 3–4, SV 6910-8

Name _____  Date _____

# Where Can You Find Air Pollution?

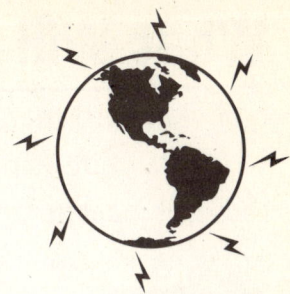

When a piece of wood is burned, carbon dioxide, ash, tar, and carbon are released into the air. Cars burn gasoline in their engines. The exhaust contains products that also cause pollution. Air pollution is harmful to plants, animals, and people. Where is air pollution most common where you live? Do this experiment to find out.

### MATERIALS

magnifying glass    1 sheet of white paper
petroleum jelly    3 plastic squares (about 1 in. x 2 in.)
a crayon

## PROCEDURE

1. With the crayon, label the squares **A**, **B**, and **C**.
2. Use your finger to coat each square with a thin layer of petroleum jelly.
3. Put square **A** in a drawer. Put square **B** on a windowsill in your classroom. Put square **C** on a windowsill outdoors.
4. Leave the squares for 24 hours. Then collect them. Put them on the white paper and examine them with the magnifying glass.

## DRAWING CONCLUSIONS

1. Which square showed the most dust and dirt?
2. Which square showed the least dust and dirt?
3. Are dust and dirt in the air? Explain.
4. What could be the sources of the dust and the dirt on each plastic square?

**MORE IDEAS**

1. Tape the plastic squares on your display. Label the location of each.
2. Do research to find sources of pollution in your town.
3. Do research to find ways to control air pollution.

# What Will Rust?

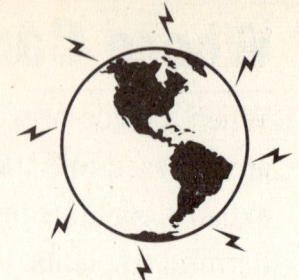

Iron is a hard metal. Some objects that contain iron will rust when they are exposed to air. You can find out what some of these objects are.

**MATERIALS**

several test items:

| | | |
|---|---|---|
| sponge | rubber bands | bottle caps |
| water | paper clips | coins |
| bowl | nails | aluminum foil |
| | staples | steel wool |

## PROCEDURE

1. Soak a sponge thoroughly with water. Set it in the bowl. Add enough water just to cover the bottom of the bowl. Make sure the water does not cover the top of the sponge.
2. Select the objects that you want to test. Place them on the sponge.
3. Set aside the sponge for 4 days. If it begins to dry out, add more water.

## DRAWING CONCLUSIONS

1. Look at the objects. On which objects did rust form?
2. Which objects contain iron?
3. Which objects do not contain iron?

## MORE IDEAS

1. Show each object in your display. Separate the objects into those that rust and those that do not rust.
2. Do research on rust. What causes rust? Why could rust be a bad thing?
3. Are there any times rust could be a good thing?

Name _____ Date _____

# Can You Take Water Out of the Air?

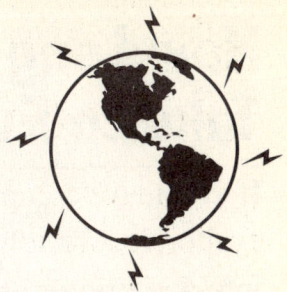

Putting water into the air is something you have done often. For example, when you wash your hair, the water doesn't stay on your hair. It evaporates. But have you ever taken the water out of the air? Water vapor is in the air. When water vapor is cooled, it collects into water droplets. Here is a way to change water vapor to liquid water.

### MATERIALS

empty metal can  spoon
water  paper towel
3 ice cubes  food coloring

### PROCEDURE

1. Fill the can halfway with cold water. Put in 3 drops of food coloring and stir. What color is the water?
2. Add the ice cubes. Wipe the outside of the can with the paper towel. Make sure the can is dry. Wait a few minutes.

### DRAWING CONCLUSIONS

1. What forms on the outside of the can? What color are the drops?
2. Did they come from inside the can? How do you know?
3. Where else have you seen water droplets collect?

**MORE IDEAS**

1. Include your setup in your display. Demonstrate your project for the judges.
2. Why do water droplets collect on a window on a cold day?
3. How is this demonstration like rain forming in clouds?

Name _____ Date _____

# How Long Does Water Take to Evaporate?

If you leave a cup of water out long enough, the water will all evaporate. What happens if you pour the same amount of water into a pie tin or a soda bottle? Does it take the same amount of time to evaporate? Does it take more or less time? Do this experiment to find out.

**MATERIALS**

| | |
|---|---|
| large paper cup | pie tin |
| measuring cup | soda bottle |
| funnel | water |

**PROCEDURE**

1. Put the paper cup, the pie tin, and the soda bottle on a table where they can stay for a week. Make sure they are out of direct sunlight and away from drafts. Fill the measuring cup with water. The cup holds 250 milliliters. Pour the water into the paper cup.
2. Pour one measuring cup of water into the pie tin. Using the funnel, pour one measuring cup into the soda bottle.
3. The next day, carefully pour the water from the paper cup into the measuring cup. Record the water level in the graph. Pour the water back into the paper cup.
4. Do the same thing with the water in the soda bottle. Use the funnel when you pour the water back into the bottle.
5. Ask an adult to help you pour the water from the pie tin into the measuring cup. Record your measurements in the graph.
6. Every day for a week, measure the water left in each container. Record your results.

Name _____ Date _____

# How Long Does Water Take to Evaporate?, page 2

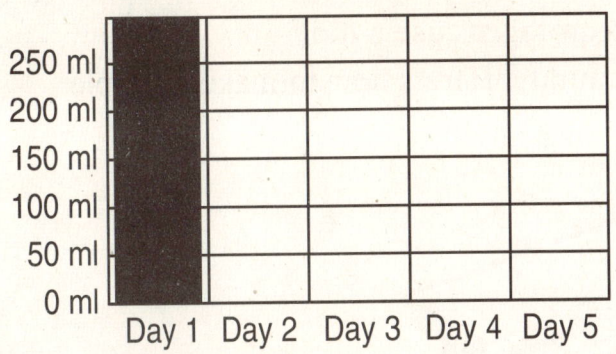
WATER LEVEL IN PAPER CUP

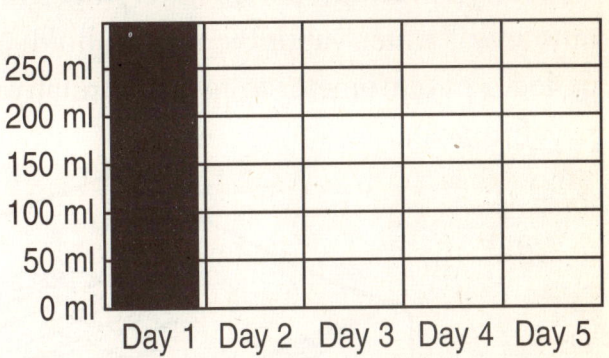
WATER LEVEL IN SODA BOTTLE

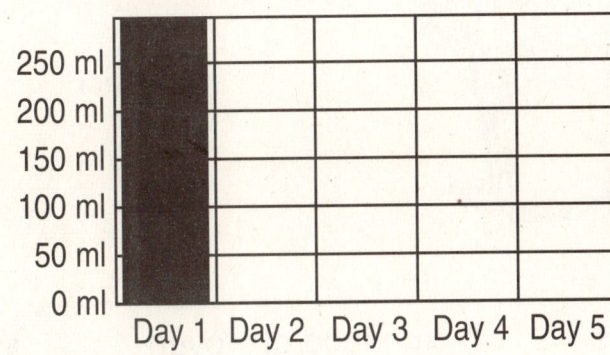
WATER LEVEL IN PIE TIN

## DRAWING CONCLUSIONS

1. From which container did the water evaporate most quickly? How long did it take?
2. From which container did the water evaporate most slowly? How long did it take?
3. How can you explain your results?

**MORE IDEAS**

1. Include the graphs in your display. Be ready to explain why the water evaporated more quickly from one container than another.
2. Do research on the water cycle. Why is evaporation important?
3. Have you ever hung clothes on a clothesline? What causes the clothes to dry?

Name _____    Date _____

# Can You Record Changes in Humidity?

Humidity is the amount of water vapor in the air. Relative humidity is the amount of water vapor in the air compared with the amount of water vapor the air can hold. Meteorologists use a tool called a psychrometer to measure relative humidity. Here's how to make a simple psychrometer.

## MATERIALS

2 Celsius thermometers
2 pieces of stiff cardboard (23 x 30 cm)
transparent tape
2 or 3 books
8-cm piece of woven shoelace (forms a tube)
small cup of water
clock

## PROCEDURE

1. Tape the two thermometers to one piece of cardboard, as shown in the diagram.
2. Lay this piece of cardboard on the books.
3. Slip the shoelace tube over the bulb of one thermometer. Let the other end of the tube hang into the cup of water under the bulb. This is the wet-bulb thermometer. The other is the dry-bulb thermometer.
4. Fan the bulbs with the other piece of cardboard. Wait until the wet-bulb temperature stays the same for a minute. Record the wet-bulb and dry-bulb temperatures.
5. Subtract the smaller number from the larger one to find the difference between the two temperatures.

# Can You Record Changes in Humidity?, page 2

**6.** Use the table below to find relative humidity. First, on the left-hand side of the chart, find the row for the dry-bulb temperature. Then, at the top of the chart, find the column for the difference between the two temperatures. The number where the row and column meet is the relative humidity.

| Dry-bulb Temp. (°C) | Difference between wet-bulb and dry-bulb temperatures (°C) |||||||||||||||||| 
|---|---|---|---|---|---|---|---|---|---|---|---|---|---|---|---|---|---|
| | 1° | 2° | 3° | 4° | 5° | 6° | 7° | 8° | 9° | 10° | 11° | 12° | 13° | 14° | 15° | 16° | 17° | 18° |
| 11° | 89 | 78 | 67 | 56 | 46 | 36 | 27 | 18 | 9 | | | | | | | | | |
| 12° | 89 | 78 | 68 | 58 | 48 | 39 | 29 | 21 | 12 | | | | | | | | | |
| 13° | 89 | 79 | 69 | 59 | 50 | 41 | 32 | 23 | 15 | 7 | | | | | | | | |
| 14° | 90 | 79 | 70 | 60 | 51 | 42 | 34 | 26 | 18 | 10 | | | | | | | | |
| 15° | 90 | 80 | 71 | 61 | 53 | 44 | 36 | 27 | 20 | 13 | 6 | | | | | | | |
| 16° | 90 | 81 | 71 | 63 | 54 | 46 | 38 | 30 | 23 | 15 | 8 | | | | | | | |
| 17° | 90 | 81 | 72 | 64 | 55 | 47 | 40 | 32 | 25 | 18 | 11 | | | | | | | |
| 18° | 91 | 82 | 73 | 65 | 57 | 49 | 41 | 34 | 27 | 20 | 14 | 7 | | | | | | |
| 19° | 91 | 82 | 74 | 65 | 58 | 50 | 43 | 36 | 29 | 22 | 16 | 10 | | | | | | |
| 20° | 91 | 83 | 74 | 66 | 59 | 51 | 44 | 37 | 31 | 24 | 18 | 12 | 6 | | | | | |
| 21° | 91 | 83 | 75 | 67 | 60 | 53 | 46 | 39 | 32 | 26 | 20 | 14 | 9 | | | | | |
| 22° | 92 | 83 | 76 | 68 | 61 | 54 | 47 | 40 | 34 | 28 | 22 | 17 | 11 | 6 | | | | |
| 23° | 92 | 84 | 76 | 69 | 62 | 55 | 48 | 42 | 36 | 30 | 24 | 19 | 13 | 8 | | | | |
| 24° | 92 | 84 | 77 | 69 | 62 | 56 | 49 | 43 | 37 | 31 | 26 | 20 | 15 | 10 | 5 | | | |
| 25° | 92 | 84 | 77 | 70 | 63 | 57 | 50 | 44 | 39 | 33 | 28 | 22 | 17 | 12 | 8 | | | |
| 26° | 92 | 85 | 78 | 71 | 64 | 58 | 51 | 46 | 40 | 34 | 29 | 24 | 19 | 14 | 10 | 5 | | |
| 27° | 92 | 85 | 78 | 71 | 65 | 58 | 52 | 47 | 41 | 36 | 31 | 26 | 21 | 16 | 12 | 7 | | |
| 28° | 93 | 85 | 78 | 72 | 65 | 59 | 53 | 48 | 42 | 37 | 32 | 27 | 22 | 18 | 13 | 9 | 5 | |
| 29° | 93 | 86 | 79 | 72 | 66 | 60 | 54 | 49 | 43 | 38 | 33 | 28 | 24 | 19 | 15 | 11 | 7 | |
| 30° | 93 | 86 | 79 | 73 | 67 | 61 | 55 | 50 | 44 | 39 | 35 | 30 | 25 | 21 | 17 | 13 | 9 | 5 |

## DRAWING CONCLUSIONS

1. What relative humidity reading did you get?
2. Predict how your classroom's relative humidity compares with the relative humidity outside. Test your prediction. How accurate was it?
3. Predict how your readings would be different outside on a rainy day. Test your prediction. How accurate was it?

**MORE IDEAS**

1. Include the chart in your display.
2. Keep a record of the humidity each day for a week. Get the weather report showing the humidity for each of those days. You can get a weather report in the newspaper or on the TV. How accurate is your psychrometer?

Name _____  Date _____

# How Can You Measure Humidity?

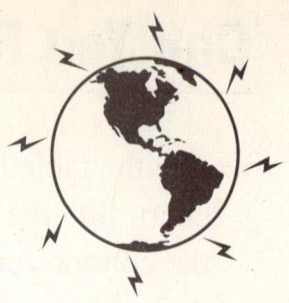

Humidity is the amount of moisture in the air. This moisture is in the form of water vapor. You can make an instrument that measures how much moisture the air contains. It is called a hair hygrometer.

### MATERIALS

- large jar lid
- cardboard (20 cm x 25 cm)
- pencil
- ruler
- tape
- thumbtacks
- straight pin
- small box or wooden block
- stiff paper
- hair (20 cm long)
- sponge
- towel
- sink or basin

## PROCEDURE

1. Using the jar lid as a guide, draw a half-circle near the bottom of the cardboard. Put 10 marks along the line, each 5 mm apart.
2. Stand the cardboard upright. Tack it to the box or wooden block.
3. Cut an arrow out of the stiff paper. Make it about 10 cm long. Using the straight pin, pin the arrow onto the cardboard so that the point swings along the half-circle. Make sure that the arrow can swing freely.
4. Tape one end of the hair to the middle of the arrow. Stretch the hair tightly, so that the arrow points near the top of the half-circle. Tape the other end of the hair to the top of the cardboard.
5. To set your hygrometer, place it in a sink or basin next to a wet sponge. Cover the sink with a damp towel.

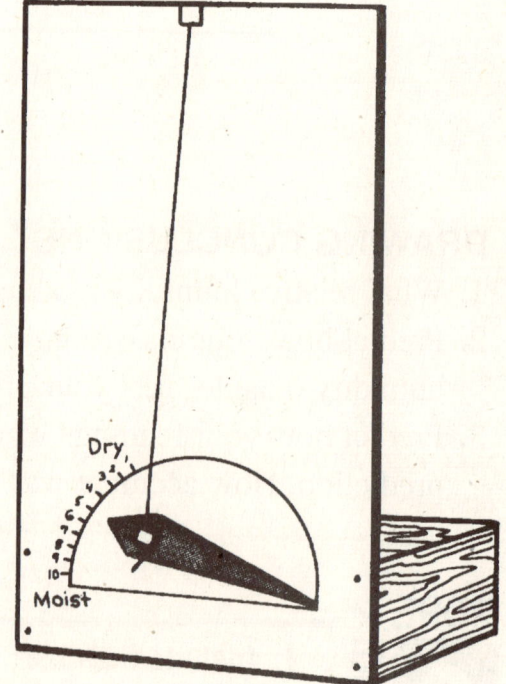

Name _____   Date _____

# How Can You Measure Humidity?, page 2

6. Leave the hygrometer for 10 minutes. Then, remove the towel. Take the hygrometer out of the sink. Quickly label the mark in front of the pointer **10**. This represents the greatest amount of water vapor in the air. Number the other marks as shown.

7. After an hour, look at the pointer. Did it change position? In the chart, record the number it is pointing to. Check the pointer at the same time every day for five days. Record the number each day.

|  | Number Arrow Pointed To | Humid or Dry Day |
|---|---|---|
| Day 1 | | |
| Day 2 | | |
| Day 3 | | |
| Day 4 | | |
| Day 5 | | |

When the air is wet, the hair gets longer. When the air is dry, the hair gets shorter. When the arrow points to the high numbers, it means the air is very humid. When it points to the low numbers, it means the air is dry. In the chart, write whether the day is dry or humid.

**MORE IDEAS**

1. Display your hair hygrometer and your results chart.
2. Watch a TV weather report to find out the current humidity. Check your hygrometer. How accurate is your hygrometer?
3. Do research to find out how humidity is related to different kinds of weather.

Name _____  Date _____

# Can Fresh Water Be Made from Salt Water?

Almost all the water on the Earth is in the ocean. And even though ocean water isn't poisonous, if you drink enough of it, you'll die of thirst. Your body will dehydrate, or dry out, as it works to get rid of the extra salt. But wouldn't it be useful if you could separate the salt from the water? Try this activity to find out if you can.

**MATERIALS**

- salt
- clear plastic cup
- very warm tap water
- spoon
- small plastic plate
- clear plastic bowl

## PROCEDURE

1. Put one spoonful of salt into the cup.
2. Add very warm water to the cup until it is half full, and stir. The salt should dissolve, or disappear, into the water.
3. Set the cup of water on the plastic plate. Put the clear plastic bowl upside down over the cup of salt water.
4. Check your setup after 15 minutes. If water has collected on the inside of the clear plastic bowl, taste it.
5. With an adult's permission, take a small sip of the water in the cup. (Drinking a small sip of salt water is not dangerous. Your body won't get any more salt than it would from eating a few crackers.)
6. Record your observations.

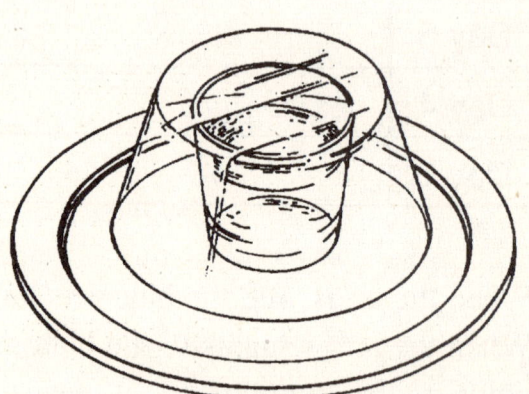

## DRAWING CONCLUSIONS

1. What did you find after 15 minutes?
2. How did the water inside the bowl taste? How did the water in the cup taste?
3. How can you explain what happened in this activity?
4. What do you think happened to the salt in the cup?
5. Why do you think it is difficult and expensive to obtain large quantities of drinking water from salt water?

Name _____  Date _____

# Is Your Water Hard or Soft?

Matter such as salt can dissolve in water. All tap water has some matter dissolved in it. If water has a lot of matter dissolved in it, it is called hard water. Water with only a little matter dissolved in it is called soft water.

### MATERIALS

liquid soap
2 jars with lids
tap water
rainwater or distilled water
$\frac{1}{4}$ teaspoon measure

## PROCEDURE

1. Put a cup of rainwater in one jar. Rainwater is soft. It has no matter dissolved in it. Label this jar **Rainwater**.
2. Put a cup of tap water in the other jar. Label this jar **Tap Water**.
3. Put exactly $\frac{1}{4}$ teaspoon of soap into each jar.
4. Cover and shake each jar. Lots of suds is a sign of soft water.

## DRAWING CONCLUSIONS

1. Did you get suds in both jars?
2. Do you have hard or soft water in your home?

### MORE IDEAS

1. Include your setup and results in your display. Do your experiment for the judges.
2. Do research to learn what happens when you bathe or wash clothes in hard water.

www.svschoolsupply.com
© Steck-Vaughn Company

Unit 1: Earth Science
Science Projects 3–4, SV 6910-8

Name _____  Date _____

# How Strong Is Surface Tension?

Surface tension is a force that occurs at the surface of a liquid. The molecules in a liquid are held together by a force. At the surface of a liquid, this force makes the surface act like an elastic film—like a thin, strong "skin." For this reason, the film can support light objects, such as insects that regularly "walk" on water. In this project, you can perform an experiment to show the strength of surface tension.

### MATERIALS

water     1 plastic cup     2 paper clips

## PROCEDURE

1. Place a nearly full cup of water on a flat surface. Make sure the surface is stable and does not shake.
2. Bend a paper clip at a right angle and use it carefully to lower another paper clip onto the surface of the water.
3. If it does not float, keep trying. Try not to upset the water's surface.
4. Can you get more than one paper clip to float?

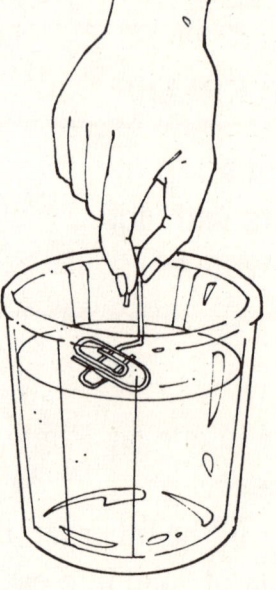

## DRAWING CONCLUSIONS

1. What does the experiment show about surface tension?
2. Can you explain why the experiment worked?
3. What happens if you upset the water's surface when you place the paper clip?

### MORE IDEAS

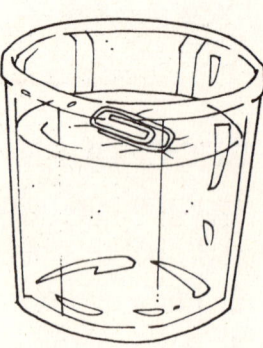

1. Do the demonstration for the judges. Include other examples of surface tension on your display.
2. Do you know how to break surface tension? Add one drop of dishwashing liquid to the cup with the floating paper clip. What happens? Why?

Name _____  Date _____

# Do Different Liquids Have Different Freezing Points?

The temperature at which a liquid turns into a solid is called its freezing point. Different liquids have different freezing points. In this project, you will investigate the freezing points of several liquids.

### MATERIALS

- 1 marking pen
- 1 tall, narrow glass container (An olive jar or baby bottle is ideal.)
- 1 plastic bowl, can, or other container, two to three times wider than the glass container
- 1 thermometer
- ice
- salt
- several test liquids, such as milk, salt water, rubbing alcohol, vinegar, and water
- record sheet

## PROCEDURE

1. First, predict the freezing point of each liquid. Make the prediction part of your hypothesis.
2. Draw a mark on the glass container to indicate the filling level (about one half to three quarters full).
3. Fill the glass container to the mark with one test liquid.
4. Set the glass container in the bowl or can.
5. Insert the thermometer vertically into the test liquid.
6. Fill the bowl or can with ice.
7. Pour salt on the ice. Be careful not to get it in your test liquid.
8. Place the setup in the freezer. Check it at 3- to 5-minute intervals, removing it as soon as it appears to begin freezing. Record its temperature.
9. Rinse the glass and dry it.
10. Repeat Steps 2 through 8 with several other test liquids. You may use the same container of ice and salt each time, adding more as needed.

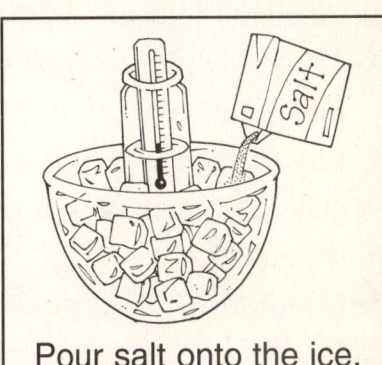

Pour salt onto the ice.

## DRAWING CONCLUSIONS

1. Did each liquid freeze at the same temperature or at different temperatures?
2. Did any of the liquids you tested freeze at the point usually considered "freezing" (32° F or 0° C)—the freezing point of pure water? How would you explain the reasons for the differences?
3. Were there any test liquids that did not freeze?

Name _____     Date _____

# Can the Freezing Point of Water Be Lowered?

Water freezes into solid ice at 32° F or 0° C. When another substance, such as salt, is added to the water before or after it freezes, the freezing point is lowered. In other words, a temperature lower than 32° F (0° C) must be reached for salt water to freeze or for a mixture of ice and salt to remain frozen. This is why salt is scattered on ice to make it melt. The salt solution has a lower freezing temperature than pure water, so the ice begins to melt. However, as the ice melts and dilutes the salt solution, it may again begin to freeze. In this project, you will investigate this event.

### MATERIALS

1 glass of cold water     salt
1 ice cube                piece of string

## PROCEDURE

1. Place the ice cube in the glass of water.
2. Try to lift the ice cube from the water with the string.
3. Lay the string over the top center of the ice cube and sprinkle salt on the string and the ice cube.
4. Count to 10, then slowly lift.
5. Or, place the ice cube on a table, lay the string across the top, and sprinkle on salt. Observe what happens.

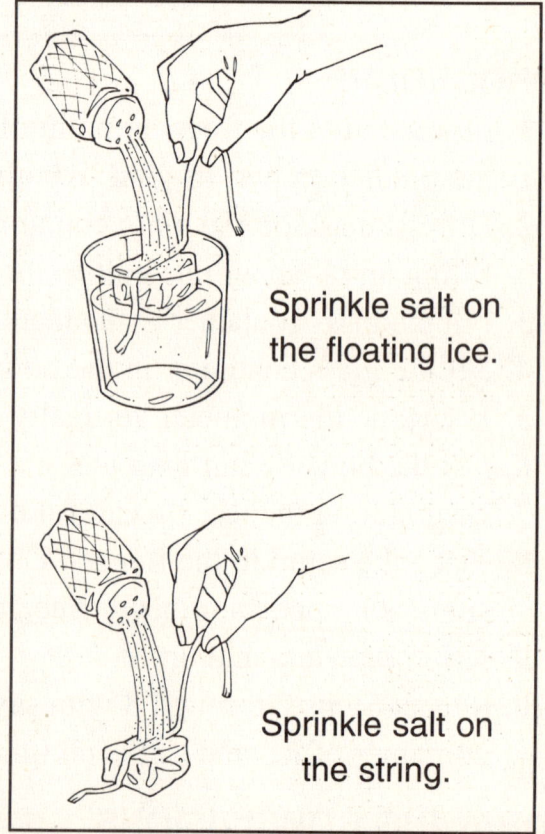

Sprinkle salt on the floating ice.

Sprinkle salt on the string.

## DRAWING CONCLUSIONS

Using what you learned in the introduction, explain why you were able to lift the ice after the salt was added but not before.

**MORE IDEAS**

1. Include your setup in your display. Do your experiment for the judges.
2. What would happen if you used something other than salt? Make a prediction. Then, try other substances, such as sugar, baking soda, or baking powder, to lower the freezing point of ice. What are the results?

# Which Heats Faster, Soil or Water?

The Sun sends heat to everything on the Earth. But does the Sun heat everything on the Earth evenly? This activity will help you show that soil and water are heated at different rates by the Sun.

## MATERIALS

2 bowls
2 thermometers
potting soil
watch or clock
water

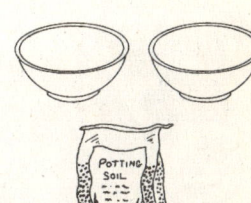

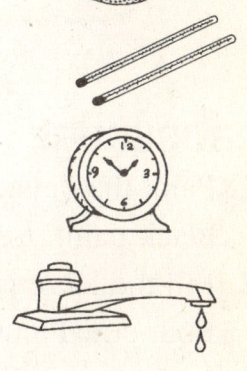

## PROCEDURE

1. Fill one bowl with water. Fill the other bowl with potting soil to the same depth.
2. Place a thermometer in each bowl. Set the bowls next to each other in direct sunlight.
3. Observe the temperature of the water and the soil when you start and then every 15 minutes up to 90 minutes. Record your observations in the chart below.

| | | | | TEMPERATURES | | | |
|---|---|---|---|---|---|---|---|
| | Start | 15 min | 30 min | 45 min | 60 min | 75 min | 90 min |
| Soil | | | | | | | |
| Water | | | | | | | |

## DRAWING CONCLUSIONS

1. Did the temperatures of the soil and the water change? By how much did each change?
2. Which heats faster, soil or water? Why?

Name _____   Date _____

# How Can You Trap the Sun's Energy?

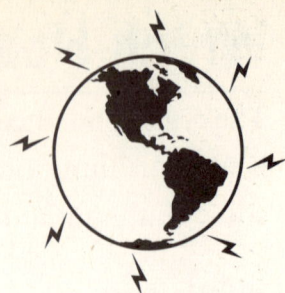

People design and build strong houses for shelter. In cold climates, they need to heat their homes, too. Some people trap the Sun's energy to warm their houses. To find out how the Sun's energy is trapped, you can make a model of a solar collector.

**MATERIALS**

| | |
|---|---|
| water | paint brush |
| black paint | 2 empty tin cans (same size) |
| large jar | thermometer |

## PROCEDURE

1. Paint the outside of one can with black paint. Let it dry.
2. Fill the large jar with cold water. Pour equal amounts of this water into both cans.
3. Place the cans side by side in a sunny spot. Make sure they are not near a radiator. Measure the temperature of water in both cans. Record your findings in the chart on the next page.
4. Measure the temperature of the air next to the cans. Record it in the chart.
5. Make sure that both cans are in the Sun all day long. Move them if necessary. After 4 hours, measure all three temperatures again. Record your findings in the chart on the next page.

# How Can You Trap the Sun's Energy?, page 2

|  | Unpainted Can | Painted Can | Air |
|---|---|---|---|
| Starting temperature |  |  |  |
| Temperature after 4 hours |  |  |  |

**DRAWING CONCLUSIONS**

1. Which was warmer, the temperature of the air or the temperature of the water at the start?
2. What happened to the water temperature in the unpainted can?
3. What happened to the water temperature in the painted can?
4. In which can did the water temperature change more?
5. Where did the heat come from that heated the water?
6. How can you explain the difference in the water temperature?

**MORE IDEAS**

1. Include your setup and chart in your display.
2. Do research on solar water-heating systems for homes. Include some pictures in your display.
3. Dark colors absorb more of the Sun's energy than do light colors. So the inside of real solar collectors is often painted black. What color clothing do you think you should wear on a hot day? Why?

Name _____  Date _____

# Is It Cooler Underground or Aboveground?

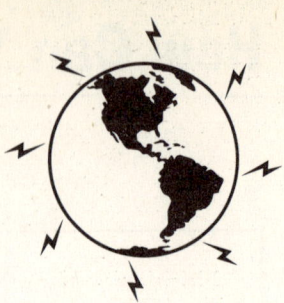

The Sun warms the air and the land. In the summer, the soil on the surface feels warm to the touch. What about the soil below the surface? Is it cooler or warmer than the soil above the ground level? Try this experiment to find out.

**MATERIALS**

2 thermometers
cardboard, 20 cm x 30 cm
spoon

## PROCEDURE

1. Dig a hole in the ground.
2. Put one thermometer in the hole.
3. Cover the hole with the sheet of cardboard.
4. Put the other thermometer on top of the cardboard.
5. Wait 30 minutes. Then, read both thermometers.

## DRAWING CONCLUSIONS

1. What is the temperature of the thermometer in the hole?
2. What is the temperature of the thermometer above the ground?
3. What is the difference between the temperatures of the thermometers?
4. Is it cooler underground or aboveground? Why do you think this is so?

**MORE IDEAS**

1. Include a drawing of your experiment and your results in your display.
2. Some people build their homes underground. Why? Do research to find out about these underground homes. Include pictures in your display.

Name _____     Date _____

# Can You Make a Cloud?

Clouds are made of many water droplets high in the sky. Clouds can drop rain, snow, sleet, or other kinds of precipitation on the Earth. Can you make a cloud in a bottle? Try this activity to find out.

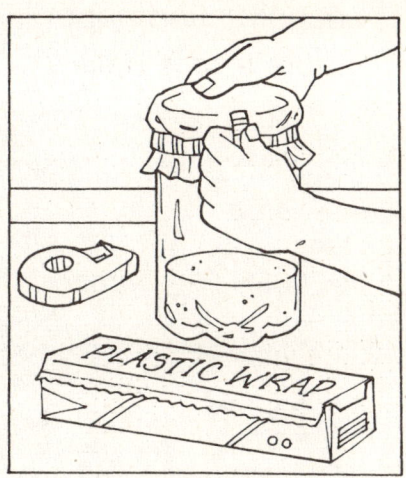 

**MATERIALS**

tape
plastic wrap
5 ice cubes

plastic bottle with the top cut off
cup of hot water

## PROCEDURE

1. Very carefully pour the cup of hot water into the bottle.
2. Cover the opening at the top of the bottle with the plastic wrap. Tape the plastic to the sides of the bottle.
3. Place 5 ice cubes on top of the plastic wrap. Then, watch the inside of the bottle.

## DRAWING CONCLUSIONS

1. What did you see under the plastic wrap?
2. What is the purpose of the ice cubes?
3. What happened to the hot water in the bottle?
4. What happened to the water vapor in the bottle?

**MORE IDEAS**

1. Include pictures of different kinds of clouds on your display.
2. Do research to find out how clouds form. How is the cloud in this experiment like a real cloud?

Name _____  Date _____

# What Does the Solar System Look Like?

The solar system contains the Sun and nine planets. You can make a model to show the relative size of each of the planets.

**MATERIALS**

| | | |
|---|---|---|
| markers | balloons | construction paper |
| tape | ruler | table tennis balls |
| clay | | |

## PROCEDURE

1. Color a table tennis ball blue. Write "Earth" on it. Color another table tennis ball light green. Write "Venus" on it.
2. Blow up an orange balloon until it is about 17 inches across. Write "Jupiter" on it. Blow up a yellow balloon until it is about 15 inches across. Write "Saturn" on it. Use construction paper to make a ring.
3. Blow up a light-blue balloon until it is about 6 inches across. Write "Uranus" on it. Blow up a dark-blue balloon until it is about 6 inches across. Write "Neptune" on it.
4. Make a ball of red clay $\frac{3}{4}$ inch across. Write "Mars" on it. Make a ball of blue clay $\frac{1}{3}$ inch across. Write "P" on it to stand for Pluto. Make a ball of red clay $\frac{1}{2}$ inch across. Write "M" on it for Mercury.

## DRAWING CONCLUSIONS

1. How are the inner planets like the outer planets? How are they different?
2. Which planet is the largest? Which is the smallest?
3. Which planet is about the same size as Earth?

## MORE IDEAS

1. Include your planet models with your display.
2. Do research to find out the distance of each planet from the Sun. Then, draw a diagram to show the position of each planet and its distance from the Sun.

Name _____   Date _____

# How Much Would You Weigh on Other Planets?

The planets are different sizes. Some are larger than Earth. Some are smaller. Their gravitational pulls are different, too. If you could go to the planets, you would have a different weight on each one. On Mars, for example, the gravitational pull is 38 percent of that on Earth. So, on Mars your weight would be about one third your Earth weight.

To find out exactly how weight changes, try this. Suppose you weigh 30 kilograms, or about 66 pounds. What would you weigh on Mars?

1. Mars has a surface gravity of 38%.
2. Change 38% to 0.38.
3. Multiply 30 kilograms × 0.38 = 11.4 kilograms, or about 25 pounds
4. Complete the chart below.

| Planet | Surface gravity compared with Earth | Weight of child who weighs 30 kilograms on Earth |
|---|---|---|
| Mercury | 28% | |
| Venus | 85% | |
| Mars | 38% | 11.4 kg |
| Jupiter | 260% | |
| Saturn | 120% | |
| Uranus | 110% | |
| Neptune | 140% | |

The surface gravity of Pluto is not known.

## DRAWING CONCLUSIONS

1. On which planet would you probably weigh the least?
2. On which planet would you weigh the most?
3. On which planets would you weigh more than you weigh on Earth?
4. On which planets would you weigh less than you weigh on Earth?

**MORE IDEAS**
1. Include your chart with your display.
2. Do research to learn why there is a difference in gravity on the planets.

Name _____  Date _____

# Is the Earth Really Moving?

Day and night. Night and day. The Earth is always turning. You cannot see it turn. You cannot feel it turn. How can you show that the Earth moves?

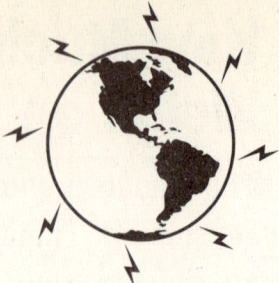

**MATERIALS**

pencil  
piece of clay  
ruler or a stick  
large sheet of white paper  
4 large rocks

## PROCEDURE

1. Go outside on a sunny morning. Put the paper on a flat surface like a sidewalk. Pick a place where the Sun will shine on the paper all day. Hold the paper down with rocks.
2. Roll the clay into a ball and place it in the middle of the paper. Push the ruler into the middle of the clay so that it stands straight up.
3. Draw the shadow of the ruler. Write the time next to the shadow. Do this once an hour until sundown.

## DRAWING CONCLUSIONS

1. What made the shadow?
2. Did the shadow change? How?
3. Why did the shadow change?
4. The Sun does not really move across the sky. It just appears to move. What is really moving?

## MORE IDEAS

1. Include your setup with your display.
2. Do research to find out how far the Earth moves each year in its orbit around the Sun.

Name _____  Date _____

# Life Science Project

A science fair project can help you to understand the world around you better. Choose a topic that interests you. Then, use the Scientific Method to develop your project. Here's an example:

1. **PROBLEM:** How do different animal traits help them to survive?

2. **HYPOTHESIS:** Animals have developed different traits that help them survive in their own environment.

3. **EXPERIMENTATION:** Research and observe different animals to see how they get their food and how they interact with their environments. Observe the animals' beaks, claws, fur, color, size, and other characteristics and behavior.

4. **OBSERVATION:** Animals have different traits that help them to catch food, to eat their food, to hide from enemies, and to stay warm in cold weather.

5. **CONCLUSION:** Animals develop the traits they need to survive in their environment.

6. **COMPARISON:** Conclusion agrees with hypothesis.

7. **PRESENTATION:** Display pictures and any live animals you have that will demonstrate the traits you have studied. Label all your displays and tell why each trait is important to animal survival.

8. **RESOURCES:** Tell of any reading you did to help you with your experiment. Tell who helped you to get materials or set up your experiment.

1. How do animals know when and where to migrate?
2. How do changes in the environment affect animal survival?
3. Can animals survive when put into a different environment?

Name _____  Date _____

# How Do Plants Get Water?

Some plants get the water they need through tubes in their stems. Some plants do not have tubes. How do they get water? To find out, compare a celery stalk with a mushroom.

### MATERIALS

| | |
|---|---|
| red or blue food coloring | mushroom |
| paper cups | toothpicks |
| water | knife |
| celery stalk | magnifying glass |

### PROCEDURE

1. Fill both cups $\frac{2}{3}$ full with water. Add a few drops of food coloring to each cup.
2. Ask an adult to help you cut a thin slice off the bottom of the celery stalk. Put the celery stalk in one of the cups.
3. Ask an adult to help you cut a thin slice off the bottom of the mushroom stem. Put four toothpicks into the cap of the mushroom. Then, put it into the other cup.
4. Leave the celery and mushroom in the water overnight.
5. The next day, ask an adult to help you cut the stems in half. Observe them with the magnifying glass. Then, fill in the chart.

| | Celery | Mushroom |
|---|---|---|
| Does the stem have spots of colored water in it? | | |
| Where is the water in the stem? | | |
| Does the plant have tubes? | | |

### DRAWING CONCLUSIONS

1. How does the celery get its water?
2. How does the mushroom gets its water?
3. What other ways can you think of that plants can get water?

Name _____  Date _____

# How Much Water Is in Fruits and Vegetables?

The water that plants take in helps them to grow. But just how much of a fruit or vegetable is water? This activity will help you to find out.

**MATERIALS**

paper
scale (optional)
variety of fruits and vegetables such as potato, apple, or orange slices, lettuce or spinach leaves

## PROCEDURE

1. If you have a scale, find the weight of each piece of food. Record this data in the chart.
2. Place the fruit and vegetable slices on a piece of paper. With a pencil, trace their shape.
3. Carefully move the paper to a dry place. Make sure that the slices stay inside their outlines. Set them aside for 3 days.
4. After the fruits and vegetables have dried, compare their sizes and shapes with their outlines. What happened?
5. If you weighed the fruits and vegetables at the start, do so again. Record your results in the chart. Compare the weight of each dried piece of food with its weight at the start. What do you find?

| Vegetable or Fruit | Weight at start | Weight at end |
|---|---|---|
|  |  |  |
|  |  |  |
|  |  |  |

## DRAWING CONCLUSIONS

1. What percentage of the weight of the fruit or vegetable was water?
2. Why do you think the fruits and vegetables changed as they dried?

Name _____ Date _____

# Can You Grow Plants Without Seeds?

When you think about growing new plants, you probably think of seeds. Yet you don't always need seeds to grow new plants. If you cut a stem that has a couple of leaves and put the stem in water, it will grow roots. Then, you can plant it in soil.

When farmers grow new potato plants, they cut up old potatoes and plant the pieces. Each piece has an eye, or small bud. Each potato eye sprouts into a new potato plant.

Many root foods that we eat, such as carrots, will grow without seeds as well. You just need to know what to do. You may have never seen the stems and leaves of a carrot plant. That's because the stems and leaves are torn from the root before the carrot is delivered to the store. However, carrots do grow leaves, stems, and even flowers. Then, they produce seeds.

You may never see a carrot flower, because carrots are biennials. That means they take two years to go through their whole life cycle and produce flowers. Carrot roots are pulled up after one growing season to be sold as food, so the plants don't get a chance to bloom.

Here's a simple way to grow a plant from a vegetable root. You can use carrots or other roots.

### MATERIALS

large carrot, beet, turnip, parsnip, radish, or rutabaga
knife (Have an adult help you.)
ruler
gravel
pie plate
water

# Can You Grow Plants Without Seeds?, page 2

## PROCEDURE

1. Ask an adult to help you cut off the top of your vegetable. Leave 5 cm of vegetable below the growing tip.
2. Pour a layer of gravel into the pie plate.
3. Push the vegetable top into the gravel. Make sure the cut side is down.
4. Pour water into the pie plate until it reaches a level of about 1.5 cm.
5. Put the pie plate on a windowsill. Watch it over the next week or two. Make sure there is always water in the bottom of the pie plate. Wait for the leaves to grow.

## DRAWING CONCLUSIONS

1. Why are carrot flowers a rare sight?
2. Could you make your carrot plant produce flowers? If so, what would you need to do?
3. Is your plant the same plant that would grow from seeds? Which method would take longer?

**MORE IDEAS**

1. Include your plant with your display.
2. Try to grow a variety of plants from roots.
3. Describe the differences in the stems and leaves grown by the different roots you use.

Name _____  Date _____

# Can You Grow Plants Without Soil?

Hydroponics is a way of gardening without soil. Plants need certain minerals from the soil in order to grow. If the minerals are supplied to the plant in water, soil is not necessary. Some vegetable and flower growers have used hydroponic gardening for many years.

Plants can be grown in a tray filled with gravel or crushed rock. Three or four times a day, water containing minerals is flooded over the rock. The water is then drained from the tray into a tank. The mineral water can be used again and again. Each week the water is tested to see what minerals need to be added. The chemicals most needed by plants are nitrogen, potassium, phosphorus, calcium, magnesium, sulfur, and iron.

Can you grow plants without soil? Try growing some plants using the hydroponic method.

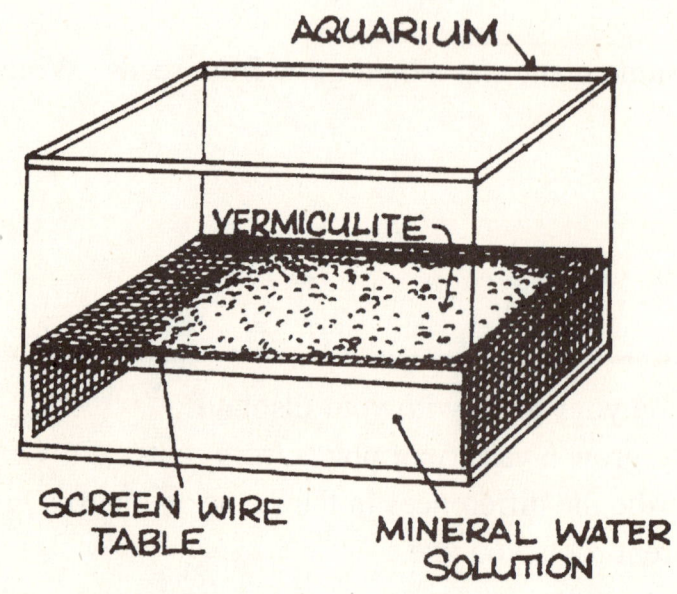

### MATERIALS

- a small aquarium
- a piece of fine mesh wire screen (the same width as the aquarium and 10 cm longer)
- water
- vermiculite
- flower seeds
- plant food
- plastic wrap

# Can You Grow Plants Without Soil?, page 2

## PROCEDURE

1. Fold the ends of the wire screen to make a table. Place the screen wire into the bottom of the aquarium.
2. Place a layer of vermiculite over the wire-screen table.
3. Scatter a few flower seeds over the vermiculite.
4. Make a solution of water and plant food that dissolves in water.
5. Fill the aquarium with water and the mineral solution to the level of the wire screen table.
6. Cover the top of the aquarium with plastic wrap to reduce evaporation. After the seeds germinate, the roots will grow down into the water.
7. Check the water level each week and add enough mineral solution to keep it level with the wire screen.

## DRAWING CONCLUSIONS

1. Did your plants grow without soil?
2. Do the plants look as healthy as ones grown in soil?
3. What minerals are in the plant food?
4. What are some advantages of hydroponic gardening?
5. What are some disadvantages of hydroponic gardening?

 **MORE IDEAS**

1. Try growing a plant in soil the same time you grow one using hydroponics. Which grows faster? Which looks healthier?
2. Include your plant setup with your display. Include a report on hydroponics in your notebook.
3. Do some research to find out what happens to plants if these minerals are missing: iron, nitrogen, phosphorus, or magnesium.

Name _____  Date _____

# Can You Grow a Kitchen Garden?

You can grow a garden without buying seed packages. Just look in your kitchen for seeds. You will probably find many that will grow. Then, start a kitchen garden.

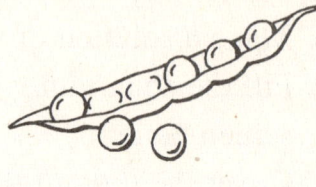

**MATERIALS**

soil    scissors    pencil    milk cartons

## PROCEDURE

1. Look for seeds in your kitchen. You may find dried beans or peas, tomato seeds, pits from ripe oranges, grapefruits, or lemons.
2. Soak the beans and peas in water overnight. The other seeds can be planted right away.
3. Cut off the tops of the milk cartons. Add soil almost to the top. Use one carton for each kind of seed.
4. In each carton, plant one large pit or several small seeds. Label each carton with the name of the seeds or pit you planted.
5. Place your cartons in a warm spot. Keep the soil moist. When shoots appear, make sure they get plenty of sunlight.
6. Use the chart to enter your results.

| What did you plant? | How many days before the shoots appeared? |
|---|---|
|  |  |
|  |  |
|  |  |

Name _____ Date _____

# Do Plants Need Light?

Photosynthesis is the process by which green plants make food. It is a complex series of chemical reactions. Plants use energy from the Sun, as well as water and carbon dioxide. In this project, you will investigate what happens to plants when they do not get sunlight.

**MATERIALS**

several live plants (You may use plants growing in your yard, but ask permission first.)

colored pencils
aluminum foil

## PROCEDURE

1. Use aluminum foil to completely cover several leaves on different plants. Make sure that the leaves are completely covered. Do this carefully, so that you do not break the leaf from the plant.
2. Wait several days and unwrap some of the leaves. Observe what has happened to them. Make a colored drawing of the leaves.
3. After several more days, unwrap the remaining leaves. Observe what has happened to them and compare them with the drawing of the leaves from Step 2.

On each plant, cover several leaves with foil.

## DRAWING CONCLUSIONS

1. Compare the color of the leaves you uncovered first with the color of the leaves that were not covered. How did they differ?
2. How did the leaves you unwrapped last compare in color with those you unwrapped first? How did their color compare with that of unwrapped leaves?
3. Why do you think this was so?

**MORE IDEAS**

1. Include your plants and drawings of the leaves with your display.
2. Try this experiment with different colors of light. Completely cover several plants with "tents" of colored cellophane (such as the cellophane used to wrap Easter baskets). How does the color of light affect plant growth? Make a hypothesis to predict how each color of cellophane might affect the plant.

Name _____  Date _____

# Do Plants Move?

Most plants stay in one place all their lives. Plant movement is usually confined to movement caused by the growth of certain structures, or parts, while the plant itself stays fixed in one place. In these two experiments, you will investigate the growth and structural movement of plants.

## MATERIALS

- water
- scissors
- cotton
- lima bean seeds
- pencils (2 per cup)
- 1 paper cup full of soil
- several seeds
- small box, taller than the paper cup
- several clear plastic cups

## EXPERIMENT 1 PROCEDURE

1. Plant several seeds in the cup of soil.
2. Keep the soil moist and observe the cup each day until plants grow to about 1 in. (2.5 cm) tall.
3. Cut a hole about the size of a quarter in one side of the box. CAUTION: Be very careful when handling the scissors or have an adult help you.
4. Set the cup of plants in a sunny spot near a window, and place the box over the cup. The hole should be facing away from the window. Wait several days and observe what happens.

## EXPERIMENT 2 PROCEDURE

1. Fill each clear plastic cup with moist cotton.
2. Place a lima bean seed in each cup between the cotton and the cup so that each bean is visible.
3. Turn each cup upside down on top of 2 pencils, leaving a space between the cup rim and the surface that the pencils are resting on. Keep the cotton moist and observe each day.

Support the cup on 2 pencils.

## DRAWING CONCLUSIONS

1. In Experiment 1, why did the plants grow toward the hole? What would happen if you turned the hole toward the window? Try it.
2. In Experiment 2, what did you learn about the direction in which plants grow?

**MORE IDEAS**

1. Include your setup with your display.
2. Investigate how the amount of light affects the way plants grow. How does light affect the growth of stems, leaves, and roots? How does the amount of light affect plant movement?

Name _____ Date _____

# How Do Plants Protect Soil?

Without plants growing in it, soil can erode. Ground cover prevents the soil from being washed away in the rain. In this activity, you will see how ground cover works.

**MATERIALS**

jar lid           fine, dry soil
leaves         2 sheets of white paper
water          eyedropper

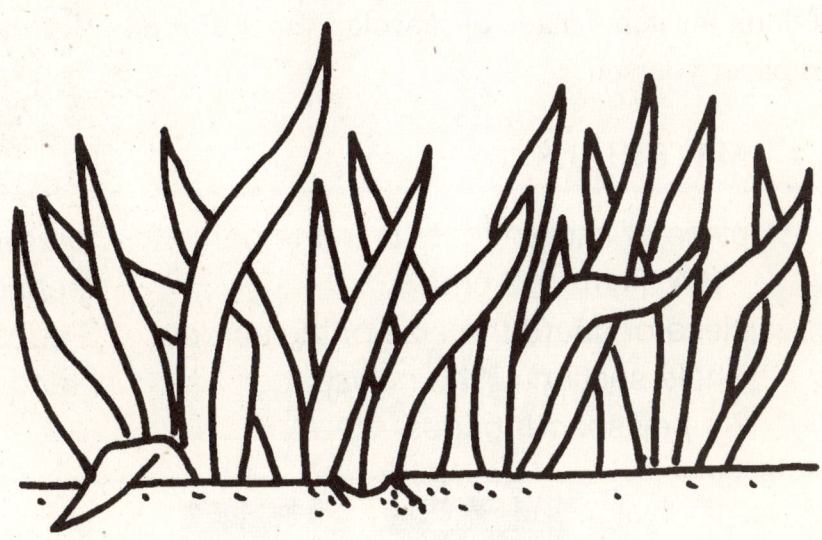

## PROCEDURE

1. Fill the jar lid with soil. Place it on a sheet of paper.
2. Fill the eyedropper with water. Hold it about 40 cm above the lid. Slowly squeeze out the water. What happens to the paper?
3. Place the lid on a second sheet of paper. Cover the soil with leaves. Then repeat Step 2. What happens to the paper now?

## DRAWING CONCLUSIONS

1. Why is the second result different from the first?
2. How can the roots of plants prevent erosion?

1. Include your setup with your display. Perform your experiment for the judges.
2. Do research to learn about more ways to control erosion.

# Can You Make Paper?

The paper in this book was once part of a tree. So was the paper in all of the books, notebooks, newspapers, magazines, tissues, boxes, and wrappers you have used all day. That's a lot of paper. In fact, you use about 275 kilograms (about 6,00 pounds) of paper each year—just by yourself. Put what you use together with what millions of other people use, and that's a lot of trees!

Recycling means using the same thing over again. Recycling paper means that fewer trees must be cut down. That saves forests from destruction. It also preserves the homes of animals and plants that live in forests.

When you shop, look for items made of recycled paper. For now, try this recipe for making recycled paper yourself.

### MATERIALS

- piece of screen that fits in the pan (14.5 cm x 12 cm)
- piece of board the size of the screen
- whole section of the newspaper
- 2 ½ newspaper pages
- large plastic pan
- measuring cup
- 5 cups of water
- blender

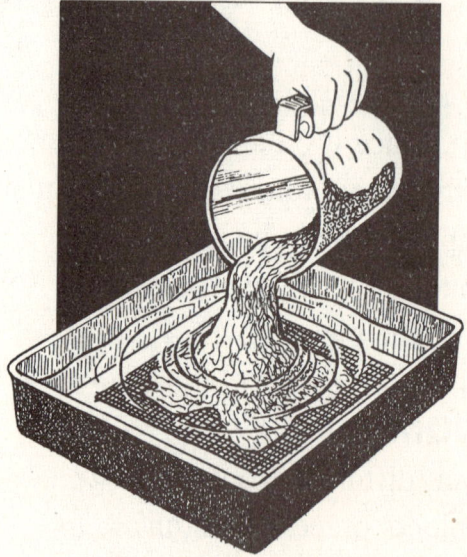

## PROCEDURE

1. Rip the 2 ½ pages of newspaper into small pieces. Put them into the blender.
2. Pour 5 cups of water into the blender. Cover the blender and turn it on for a few seconds.
3. Place the screen in the pan. Pour 1 cm of water into the bottom of the pan.

# Can You Make Paper?, page 2

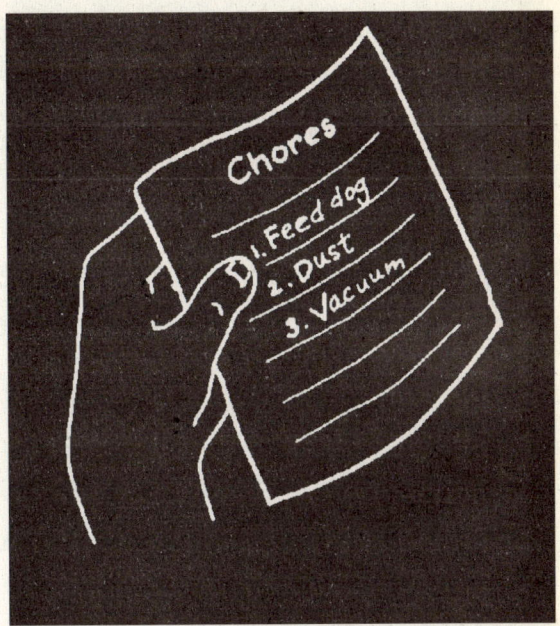

4. Pour a cup of the mush onto the screen. Spread it evenly. Lift out the screen and let the water drain off. (This will make enough for 4 to 5 sheets of recycled paper.)
5. Open up the newspaper section and place it on the table. Place the pulp-covered screen in the middle of one side of the newspaper section. Fold the newspaper section closed around it.
6. Keeping the newspaper closed, turn it over so the screen inside is on top of the paper mush. Put the newspaper on a table.
7. Put the board on the newspaper and press down to squeeze out the water. Open the newspaper. Remove the screen. Let the mush dry. This takes at least a day.
8. Carefully peel off your recycled paper. It's ready to use!

## DRAWING CONCLUSIONS

1. Think about how long it took you to make one sheet of recycled paper. If it takes companies this long to make recycled paper, why do they do it?
2. What are the advantages and disadvantages of recycling paper?

 **MORE IDEAS**

1. Include your setup and sheets of homemade paper with your display.
2. Do research on other kinds of recycling. Why is recycling important?

Name _____  Date _____

# What Foods Do Insects Like?

Different kinds of animals prefer different foods. Some animals are herbivores and eat only plants. Other animals are carnivores and eat only meat. And some animals eat plants and animals. They are called omnivores. Scavengers are animals that eat only once-living material.

All of these categories—herbivore, carnivore, omnivore, and scavenger—apply to insects. Some insects eat crops, while others eat weeds, other insects, or dead, decaying materials. In this project, you will investigate the food choices of insects that live near you.

## MATERIALS

several paper plates containing a variety of foods, such as:

| banana (peeled) | bread | apple slices |
| coffee grounds | raw meat | sugar water |
| | flowers | |

(CAUTION: Always wash your hands carefully after handling raw meat.)

## PROCEDURE

1. Select a warm, sunny day to set out the plates in your yard, at school, or in a field. Set the plates about 7 in. (17.5 cm) apart.
2. Place one type of food on each paper plate. If it is a windy day, use rocks to keep the plates from blowing away.
3. Draw a chart to keep a record of your observations.
4. Sit close enough to the plates to see any activity, but not so close as to disturb any insect visitors.
5. Make a note of the types and numbers of insects and other organisms that visit each kind of food over a period of time (for example, one hour or four 15-minute intervals throughout the day).
6. Dispose of the plates and food materials when you are finished.

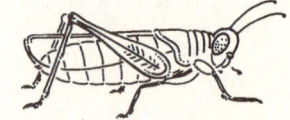

## DRAWING CONCLUSIONS

1. What food sample was visited by the most insects?
2. Did any type of insect visit more than one plate? Why do you think that this was so?
3. If you observed at different times, were there any insects that were more numerous at one time of day than another? If so, why do you think that this was so?

Name _____  Date _____

# How Does Color Protect Animals?

Many animals have colors in their skin, feathers, or fur that help them to hide from their enemies. How do colors protect these animals? Do this activity to find out.

**MATERIALS**

scissors
newspaper (filled mostly with black newsprint)
yellow construction paper

## PROCEDURE

1. Cut an equal number of small squares from the newspaper and the construction paper.
2. Spread newspaper on the floor, and scatter all of the squares on the newspaper.
3. Cover one eye with your hand.
4. Pick up squares for 10 seconds with your free hand.
5. Use the chart to record how many squares of each color you picked up.
6. Repeat Steps 3–5 two more times.

| ROUND | YELLOW SQUARES | NEWSPAPER SQUARES |
|---|---|---|
| 1 | | |
| 2 | | |
| 3 | | |
| Totals | | |

## DRAWING CONCLUSIONS

1. Which color squares did you pick up most often?
2. Which color could you see more easily? Why?
3. What does this experiment tell you about the way color can help an animal survive?

**MORE IDEAS**

1. Do this activity for the judges.
2. Do research to learn more ways that animals protect themselves from their enemies.

www.svschoolsupply.com
© Steck-Vaughn Company

Unit 2: Life Science
Science Projects 3–4, SV 6910-8

Name _____  Date _____

# How Do Animals Survive in the Cold?

The Arctic is a very cold place. Ice and snow cover the land for most of the year. Yet snowy owls and polar bears make their homes there. These animals are fit to live in the Arctic. A bear has fur to help keep it warm. An owl has down feathers. Down feathers are soft and fluffy. They are close to the bird's body. Do this activity to see how the bear and the owl keep warm.

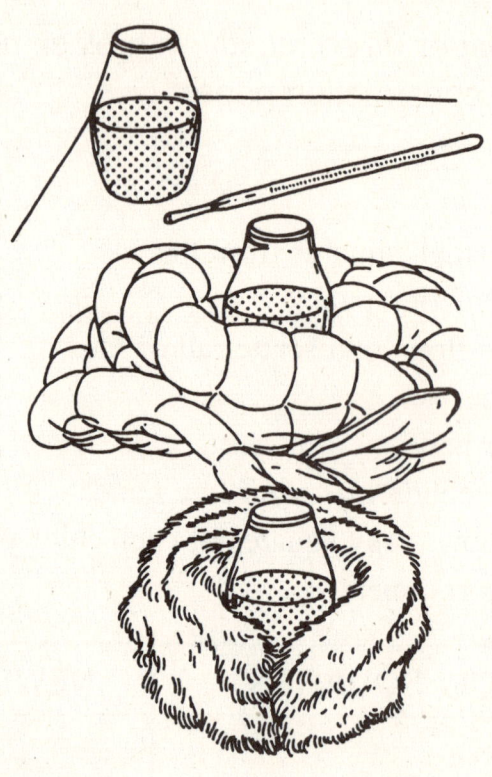

**MATERIALS**

3 jars of the same size — clock
water — down vest (or jacket)
thermometer — fur hat (or plush material)

## PROCEDURE

1. Fill each jar to the same level with very warm water. Measure the temperature of each. All 3 jars must be the same temperature. If they are not, pour out a little water from the cooler ones. Then, add hot water and stir. Keep doing this until all the jars are the same temperature. Record the starting temperature in the chart.
2. Wrap one jar in the down vest or jacket. Wrap another jar in the fur (or plush) hat. Leave the last jar uncovered.
3. Measure the temperature of each jar every 10 minutes for an hour. Record your results in the chart.

www.svschoolsupply.com
© Steck-Vaughn Company
Unit 2: Life Science
Science Projects 3–4, SV 6910-8

Name _____   Date _____

# How Do Animals Survive in the Cold?, page 2

| TIME | WATER TEMPERATURE | | |
|---|---|---|---|
| | Jar Covered with Down | Jar Covered with Fur | Uncovered Jar |
| Start | | | |
| After 10 minutes | | | |
| After 20 minutes | | | |
| After 30 minutes | | | |
| After 40 minutes | | | |
| After 50 minutes | | | |
| After 60 minutes | | | |

## DRAWING CONCLUSIONS

1. Which jar lost the most heat?
2. Which stayed warmer, the fur-covered jar or the down-covered jar?
3. How does a polar bear's fur keep it warm?
4. How does a snowy owl's down feathers keep it warm?
5. What can you wear to keep warm in cold temperatures?

**MORE IDEAS**

1. Include your setup with your display.
2. Do research to learn other ways animals protect themselves from the weather. For example, how do animals survive in the desert?

Name _____  Date _____

# How Does a Caterpillar Metamorphose?

You have probably studied the metamorphosis of some insects. You know that the caterpillar changes into a butterfly. In this activity, you will observe the changes a caterpillar undergoes.

**MATERIALS**

a large glass jar with a lid
a plastic bag
fresh leaves and twigs

CAUTION: An adult should help you punch holes in the lid of the jar.

## Procedure

1. Find a caterpillar eating a leaf. Place it into a plastic bag along with some leaves and twigs from the plant.
2. Carefully place the contents of the plastic bag into the jar.
3. Observe how the caterpillar moves and eats. If possible, watch it spin its cocoon.
4. Keep a record of how long the caterpillar takes to spin its cocoon. Then, keep track of the time until it emerges from the cocoon. Include your observations in a chart.

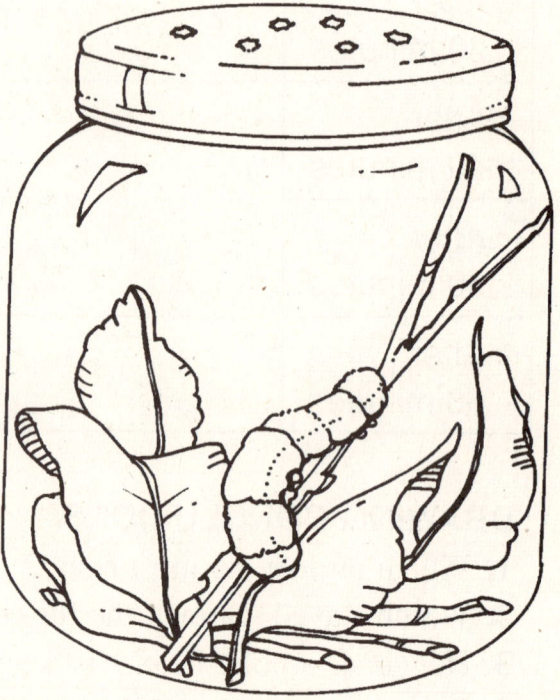

## Drawing Conclusions

1. How many legs does the caterpillar have?
2. What is the cocoon made of?
3. What is happening when the caterpillar is inside its cocoon?
4. What kind of butterfly emerges from the cocoon?

**MORE IDEAS**

1. Try collecting caterpillars from different plants. Do different kinds of butterflies emerge?
2. Try feeding different foods to the same kind of caterpillars. Do changes in food affect the development or appearance of the butterfly?

Name _____ Date _____

# How Can You Keep Cool on a Hot Day?

On hot days when the humidity is low, perspiration can evaporate from your skin. This makes you feel cooler. To see why, try this experiment.

## MATERIALS

2 thermometers       fan (optional)
2 cotton balls       water
tray                 rubber bands

## PROCEDURE

1. Dip one cotton ball in warm water. Squeeze out the excess water. Wrap the wet cotton around the bulb of the first thermometer. Wrap the bulb of the second thermometer with a dry cotton ball. Hold the cotton in place with rubber bands.
2. Record the temperature of the thermometers.
3. Set thermometers next to each other on the tray. Put the tray in front of the fan or outside in a windy place.
4. Set aside the thermometers in the tray for 30 minutes. Remove them and immediately record their temperatures below.

| Temperature of thermometers at the beginning: |
| Temperature of thermometer with wet cotton: |
| Temperature of thermometer with dry cotton: |

## DRAWING CONCLUSIONS

1. Which thermometer had the lower temperature?
2. Why did this happen?

Liquid water molecules from the wet cotton evaporated. They moved into the air and became water vapor. It takes energy for water to evaporate. The evaporating water took heat energy from the thermometer. The thermometer became cooler because it lost heat energy.

When the perspiration on your skin evaporates, you feel cooler for the same reason. The evaporating water is taking up heat energy from your body.

Name _____  Date _____

# How Do Your Heart and Lungs Work?

The heart and the lungs are two vital organs of the body. The heart, which is part of the circulatory system, is responsible for pumping the blood through this system. When you hear your heart beat, you hear your heart's valves open and close as blood enters and exits them. Lungs are a part of the respiratory system. They are the organ through which oxygen enters the body. They expand to fill with air with the help of a special muscle below them called the diaphragm. In this project, you will make an instrument to listen to your heartbeat, and construct a model of the lungs and diaphragm.

**MATERIALS**

- 1 funnel or the top cut off a plastic bottle
- rubber tubing (about 18 in. or 45 cm long)
- masking tape
- scissors
- 1 clear plastic cup
- 2 flexible drinking straws
- 2 small balloons
- modeling clay
- 1 large balloon
- 1 rubber band

## EXPERIMENT 1 PROCEDURE

1. Ask an adult to help you cut the top $\frac{1}{3}$ off the bottle to make a funnel.
2. Place one end of the rubber tubing over the end of the funnel or the bottle top. (Split the tubing and tape it, if necessary. CAUTION: Be careful when handling the scissors.)
3. Place the other end of the tubing to your ear.
4. Set the funnel over your heart. Move it around until you can hear a strong heartbeat.
5. Use your funnel "stethoscope" on other people. If you use it with a variety of age groups, old and young, you should hear a variety of heart rates.

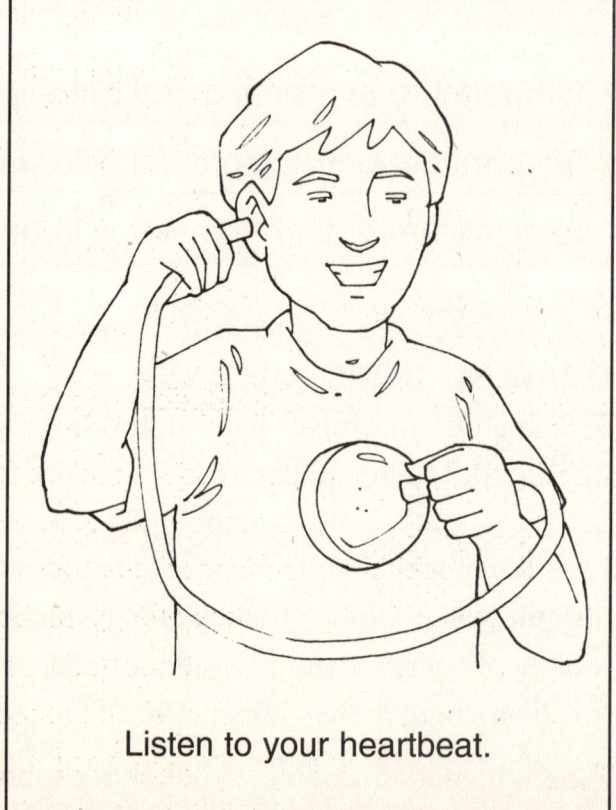

Listen to your heartbeat.

www.svschoolsupply.com
© Steck-Vaughn Company

Unit 2: Life Science
Science Projects 3–4, SV 6910-8

Name _____ Date _____

# How Do Your Heart and Lungs Work?, page 2

**EXPERIMENT 2 PROCEDURE**

1. Carefully make a hole with the scissors in the bottom center of the clear plastic cup. CAUTION: Be careful when handling the scissors.
2. Push the bottom end of a straw into the hole, from the inside of the cup outward.
3. Carefully use the scissors to cut a small vertical slit in the bend of the straw.
4. Cut a piece from the other straw the same length as the section of the first straw above the slit. (See the diagram.)
5. Slip the cut piece into the slit of the first straw. Tape it to make it airtight. Your straws should form a Y.
6. Slip one of the small balloons on each side of the Y, and tape them to make them airtight.
7. Tape the bottom of the Y of the straw to make it airtight.
8. Push the balloons up into the cup until the slit is almost even with the hole in the cup. Use modeling clay around the hole to make it airtight.
9. Cut the end off the large balloon.
10. Stretch the balloon over the opening (top) of the cup. Secure it with a rubber band and pull it tight. This balloon represents your diaphragm.
11. Hold up your model lung with one hand, with the exposed straw on top and the diaphragm on the bottom.
12. Using your thumb and index finger, pinch the diaphragm balloon and pull it down. Observe what happens.

How to make a Y-shaped tube

The completed model lung

**DRAWING CONCLUSIONS**

1. When you used your stethoscope, did you find that your heart is located where you expected it to be?
2. How did your heart rate differ from those of other people?
3. How is a doctor's stethoscope different from yours?
4. With your lung model, what did you observe when you pulled on the diaphragm? Why do you think this was so?

**MORE IDEAS**

1. Include your setup with your display.
2. Do research to learn about different diseases of the heart and lungs.

Name _____  Date _____

# How Does Activity Affect a Person's Pulse Rate?

When a person is active for an extended period of time, his or her pulse rate will become faster. When a person is inactive, his or her pulse rate will slow. When people are more active, they breathe faster, they have more color in their faces, and their pulse rates go higher. When they are inactive, they are paler, and their breathing is more regular. Do this experiment to demonstrate these facts.

### MATERIALS

watch or clock          recording chart

|  | Pulse rate at rest | After running | At rest after running |
|---|---|---|---|
| Person 1 |  |  |  |
| Person 2 |  |  |  |
| Person 3 |  |  |  |

### PROCEDURE

1. Take a person's pulse rate at rest. You can take the pulse rate at the person's wrist or chest. Record it in the chart.
2. Have the person run in place for 1 minute. Take the pulse rate again. Record it in the chart.
3. Let the person rest for 2 minutes. Take the pulse rate again. Record it in the chart.

### DRAWING CONCLUSIONS

1. Did the person's pulse rate increase after running?
2. Did the person's pulse rate go down after resting after running?
3. How does exercise affect a person's pulse rate?

### MORE IDEAS

1. Display your records and any pictures or drawings you did with your observations. Show your findings with a chart or graph.
2. Do several experiments with several different people of the same age group. Take each person's pulse before and after each activity.
3. Experiment with different lengths of time. For example, for a running-in-place activity, you might see how 1 minute of running affects the pulse rate. After letting the person rest, see if 2 minutes of running affects him or her differently. Keep careful records of all your findings.

Name _____  Date _____

# How Are Reflexes Related to Reaction Time?

A reflex is an automatic action in response to a stimulus. Doctors often test a person's reflexes to make sure his or her nervous system is working properly. In this project, you will conduct a test for reflex speed, or reaction time.

### MATERIALS

1 ruler (marked in centimeters)    record sheet
several test subjects

## PROCEDURE

1. Grip the end of the ruler with your thumb and index finger and hold it vertically.
2. Have a partner hold his or her hand directly below the ruler. Release the ruler. Have your partner catch it with his or her thumb and index finger as soon as you release the ruler. (Have your partner try catching the ruler several times before testing.)

| Distance to nearest cm | Reflex time in seconds |
|---|---|
| 1 | 0.045 |
| 2 | 0.064 |
| 3 | 0.078 |
| 4 | 0.090 |
| 5 | 0.101 |
| 6 | 0.110 |
| 7 | 0.119 |
| 8 | 0.127 |
| 9 | 0.135 |
| 10 | 0.142 |

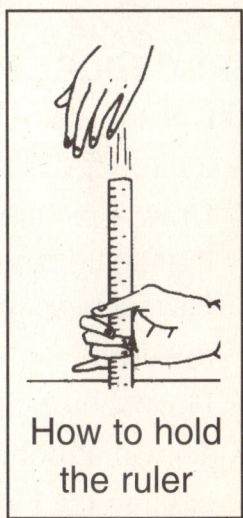

How to hold the ruler

3. Record the centimeter mark your partner is touching when the ruler is caught. Use the chart to convert the distance to a time in seconds. For the best results, do several tests with the same partner and calculate the average reflex time.
4. Test several other people and record their average reaction times.

## DRAWING CONCLUSIONS

1. Which of you had the fastest reflex time? Who had the slowest?
2. How do you think the time would differ if you used your other hand?

**MORE IDEAS**

1. Do the test for the judges. Have a judge volunteer to do the test. Point out how the judge's results compare with others you tested.
2. Expand this project by investigating if age, gender (male or female), or changing hands affects reflex time.

Name _____  Date _____

# What Is an Optical Illusion?

An optical illusion is a false impression in the brain of what the eyes are seeing. The best-known optical illusions involve shape and size, but position, color, and movement can also be misleading. Illusions of movement may occur when the eye is misled by a series of events happening one after the other. In this project, you will construct a thaumatrope. A thaumatrope is an example of an optical illusion caused by movement.

### MATERIALS

| posterboard | markers | 2 rubber bands |
| scissors | hole punch | |

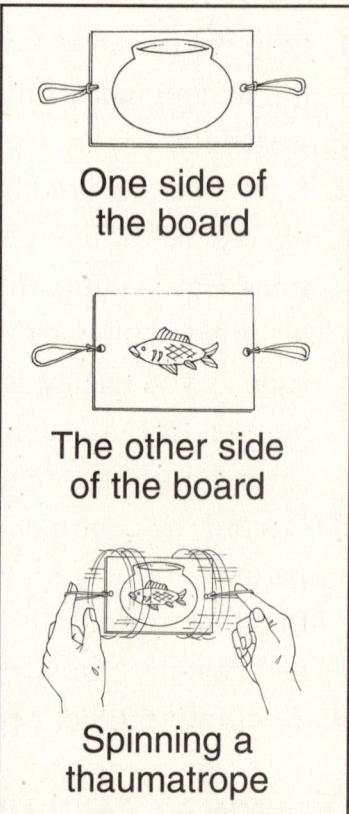

One side of the board

The other side of the board

Spinning a thaumatrope

## PROCEDURE

1. Cut a piece of posterboard about 2 in. by 3 in. (5 cm by 8 cm). CAUTION: Be careful when handling the scissors.
2. Draw a picture on each side of the posterboard, as shown in the diagrams. You may try other pictures, such as a bird and a cage. Be sure both pictures are large and centered.
3. Punch a hole in each side of the card.
4. Thread a rubber band through each hole and knot it by passing the loop on one side of the hole through the loop on the other side.
5. Slip your index fingers through each loop and wind the rubber band as tight as possible. Release and observe what happens.

## DRAWING CONCLUSIONS

1. What did you see as the card turned? Why?
2. Try winding the rubber band even tighter. As you release it, also apply more tension by pulling your fingers apart. Does the illusion change when you spin it faster? When you spin it slower? Try it.

### MORE IDEAS

1. Include your thaumatrope with your display. Demonstrate the illusion for the judges. Explain why it happens.
2. Do research to find other kinds of optical illusions. Include pictures of these in your display.

Name _____  Date _____

# Can You Find Fat in Foods?

Do you know which foods contain fats? Fats are found in a lot of different foods. Sometimes you can't see fats. For example, there is fat in milk, meat, and eggs. You can do this test to find fat in foods.

**MATERIALS**

a brown paper bag          several different foods to test
scissors

## PROCEDURE

1. Cut the paper bag into 3-inch squares. Write the name of each food you wish to test on a different square.
2. Rub a piece of food on a square until it leaves a wet spot. If the food is liquid, put a drop of it on the square.
3. Set aside the squares to dry.
4. When the squares are dry, hold them up to the light. If there is a greasy spot, the food contains fat. Fill in the chart below.

| FOOD | FAT | NO FAT |
|---|---|---|
|  |  |  |
|  |  |  |
|  |  |  |
|  |  |  |

**MORE IDEAS**

1. Include your results in your display.
2. Do research to learn if fat is healthy or unhealthy.

Name _____ Date _____

# What Happens to Dead Organisms?

Decomposers are an important part of the life cycle. Do this activity to see how decomposers break down dead organisms.

### MATERIALS

2 banana slices                powdered yeast
2 plastic sandwich bags

## PROCEDURE

1. Place a slice of banana into each bag.
2. Sprinkle some yeast onto one of the slices.
3. Close the bags tightly. Mark the bag with the yeast in it.
4. Watch the bags for 5 days. Write your observations about the differences between the two banana slices.

Day 1: _____

Day 2: _____

Day 3: _____

Day 4: _____

Day 5: _____

## DRAWING CONCLUSIONS

1. How do you know that yeast is a decomposer?
2. Write a paragraph describing what happened to the banana slices. Explain how you know that yeast is a decomposer.
3. A squirrel dies in the forest. What will happen to the squirrel?

## MORE IDEAS

1. Include your setup and results with your display.
2. Make a diagram showing a decomposer ➡ producer ➡ consumer cycle. Include these labels in your diagram: a. plants and animals die; b. decomposers break down dead organisms; c. materials return to the soil and are used by plants to make new food; d. animals eat plants.
3. Mold is another decomposer. Put foods such as bread, cheese, a banana peel, and a piece of tomato in separate plastic bags. Place the bags in a moist, warm, dark place. What happens to the food in the bags?

Name _____ Date _____

# Physical Science Project

A science fair project can help you to understand the world around you better. Choose a topic that interests you. Then, use the Scientific Method to develop your project. Here's an example:

1. **PROBLEM:** What part of a magnet holds the most?

2. **HYPOTHESIS:** The poles of a magnet have more magnetic force.

3. **EXPERIMENTATION:** Materials: different shaped magnets, paper clips, centimeter ruler
   - Find out how many paper clips the poles of each magnet will hold.
   - Find out how many paper clips the center of each magnet will hold.
   - Measure the strength of each magnet. Place a paper clip at one end of the ruler and the end of a magnet at the other. Slowly slide the magnet closer to the paper clip. When the paper clip starts to move, read the distance it is from the magnet.
   - Repeat the above step using the center of the magnets.

4. **OBSERVATION:** The poles of the magnets attracted more paper clips. The end of the magnet was also a greater distance from the paper clip before it moved.

5. **CONCLUSION:** The poles of the magnet have the greater magnetic force.

6. **COMPARISON:** The conclusion and the hypothesis agree.

7. **PRESENTATION:** Prepare a presentation or a report to explain your results. If possible, set up the materials so that other people can try the experiment.

8. **RESOURCES:** Tell the books you used to find background information. Tell who helped you to get the materials and set up the experiment.

 **MORE IDEAS**
1. What color clothing should people wear in the summer? Use thermometers and colored fabric to experiment.
2. How do people use wind to make energy? Do research on windmills and plan a project.

Name _____  Date _____

# Do Inclined Planes Make Work Easier?

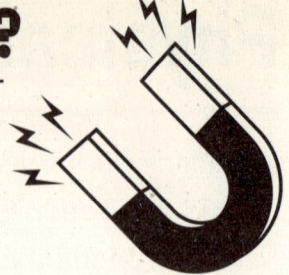

An inclined plane is an example of a simple machine. It is a flat surface that is raised at one end. It is often easier to push something up a ramp than it is to lift it the same distance, because less force is needed.

### MATERIALS

wooden board          thin spiral notebook
chair                 meter stick
masking tape          30 centimeter-long string
spring scale

## PROCEDURE

1. Place one end of the board on the edge of the chair and the other on the floor. Tape the board to the floor to hold it in place.
2. Tie one end of the string around the notebook. Tie the other end to the hook on the spring scale.
3. Place the notebook on the floor and slowly lift it straight off the ground. Read the setting on the spring scale when the notebook is no longer touching the floor. Slowly continue to lift the book until it is even with the seat of the chair. Record the number of newtons on the chart on the next page.
4. Measure the height you raised the notebook. Record the distance.

# Do Inclined Planes Make Work Easier?, page 2

5. Place the notebook on the floor at the base of the ramp. Slowly and steadily pull the spring scale up the ramp. When the notebook begins moving, read the scale. Continue to pull the notebook until it reaches the top of the ramp. Record the number of newtons needed to pull it up the ramp.
6. Measure the length of the ramp and record the distance on the chart.

### FORCE NEEDED TO MOVE OBJECT

|  | Without Ramp | With Ramp |
|---|---|---|
| Force |  |  |
| Distance |  |  |

## DRAWING CONCLUSIONS

1. Which way of moving the book took more force?
2. Which way of moving the book took a greater distance?
3. How did the ramp help to move the book?
4. How might friction affect using a ramp?

1. Include your setup in your display.
2. How are inclined ramps used in business or everyday life? Include pictures of uses of inclined planes.

Name _____  Date _____

# How Does a Lever Make Work Easier?

A lever is a simple machine made with a board or bar that moves on a fulcrum. The fulcrum is the turning point for a lever. A lever makes work easier because less force is needed to lift or move an object.

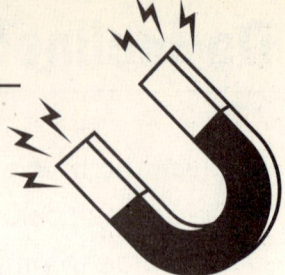

**MATERIALS**

| | |
|---|---|
| marker | 2 small paper cups |
| piece of chalk | wooden ruler, 30 cm long |
| clay | box of paper clips |
| tape | |

## PROCEDURE

1. Label one cup **L** for **Load**. Label the other cup **F** for **Force**.
2. Tape a cup to each end of the ruler.
3. Place a ball of clay on the desk. Press a piece of chalk lengthwise into the clay. It will be the fulcrum for your balance.
4. Put 10 paper clips into the **L** cup. Set the ruler on the fulcrum so that the top edge of the **L** cup is 8 cm from the chalk. Put enough paper clips in cup **F** to balance the load. It will be difficult to balance the load unless you work carefully and slowly.
5. Record your findings on the chart.
6. Remove the paper clips from cup **F**. Repeat Step 4 with cup **L** at 12 cm, at 15 cm, and at 18 cm from the fulcrum. Record your findings.

### FULCRUM AND FORCE

| Fulcrum at | Force (Number of Paper Clips) |
|:---:|:---:|
| 8 cm | |
| 12 cm | |
| 15 cm | |
| 18 cm | |

## DRAWING CONCLUSIONS

1. Did you use more or fewer paper clips as the load got farther from the fulcrum?
2. How does the position of the fulcrum affect the amount of force needed to lift a load?
3. What are some uses for a lever and fulcrum?

Name _____  Date _____

# How Do a Wheel and Axle Make Work Easier?

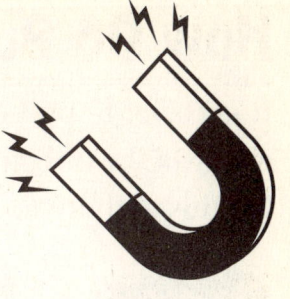

A wheel and axle is a kind of simple machine. A wheel turns on a rod when force is applied on the wheel. Even though it takes more hand movement to turn the wheel, less force is needed to do the work. Sometimes it is hard to find the wheel and axle in tools. Some examples are screwdrivers, pencil sharpeners, and fishing reels.

### MATERIALS

- 2 screwdrivers, both the same length but with different-sized handles
- 2 screws, about 2.5 cm long
- wood block
- hammer
- permanent marker

## PROCEDURE

1. Put a mark on each of the screwdriver handles so you can count the turns.
2. Lightly tap the screws into the wood to set them.
3. Use the screwdriver with the thinner handle first. Turn the screw into the block. Count how many times the handle turns as you turn the screw into the block. Record the number on the chart.
4. Now use the screwdriver with the thicker handle. Turn the second screw into the block. Count how many times the handle turns as you turn the screw into the block. Record the number on the chart.

### WHEEL AND AXLE TURNS

| Type of Screwdriver | Number of Turns |
|---|---|
| Thinner Handle | |
| Thicker Handle | |

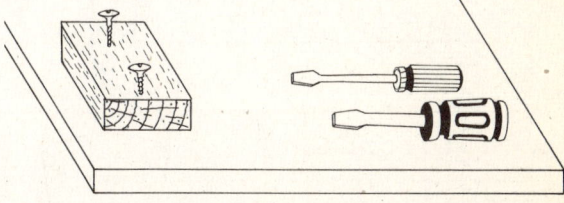

## DRAWING CONCLUSIONS

1. In what part was the wheel?
2. In what part was the axle?
3. Write a paragraph describing the difference between the two screwdrivers. Tell how the difference in their sizes affects the amount of work they can help you do.

Name _____     Date _____

# How Do Pulleys Make Work Easier?

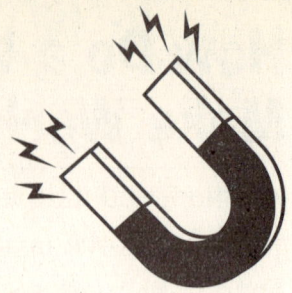

It is easier to pull or push an object than it is to lift it. A pulley changes the direction of the force so that lifting an object is easier. Do this activity to find out how.

**MATERIALS**

pail          sand       spring scale
meter stick   string     small pulley

## PROCEDURE

1. Fill the pail $\frac{1}{4}$ full with sand.
2. Lift the pail with the spring scale. Record the force needed to lift the pail on the chart.
3. Place the meter stick across two desks. Then, tie one end of the string to the meter stick. Run the string through the pulley. Tie the free end of the string to the scale.
4. Hook the pail onto the pulley. Pull on the scale to lift the pail. Record the force on the chart.

### FORCE FOR LIFTING PAIL

| Step | Force |
|------|-------|
| 2    |       |
| 4    |       |

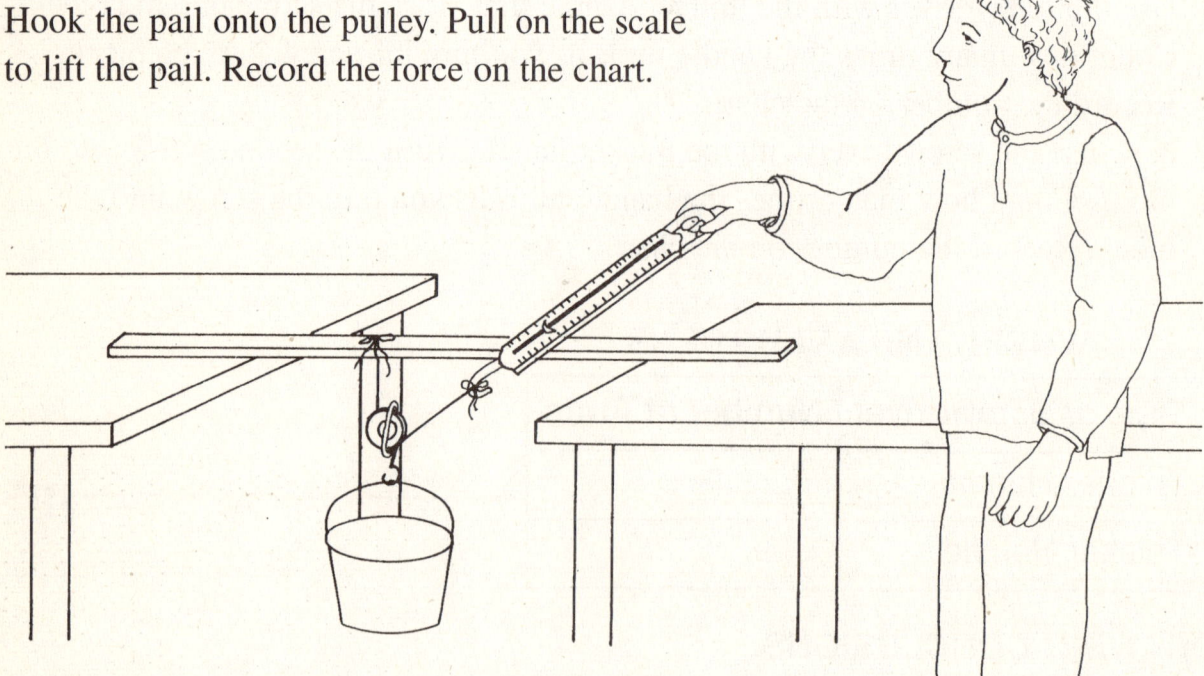

## DRAWING CONCLUSIONS

1. What kind of pulley system did you use?
2. What force was needed to lift the pail in Step 2?
3. What force was needed in Step 4?
4. How does using a pulley help make lifting an object easier?

Name _____  Date _____

# How Is Friction Affected by Different Surfaces?

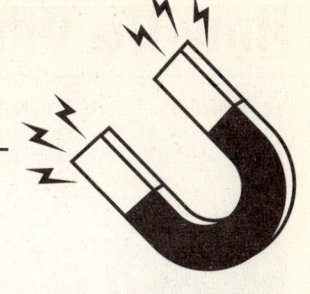

Friction is the force that affects the movement of objects. When two objects rub against each other, friction makes it harder to move them. The surface of the objects affects their movement. Smooth, flat surfaces cause less friction. Objects move more easily across each other. Rough, bumpy surfaces cause more friction. Objects with these surfaces are less likely to move.

### MATERIALS
| | | | |
|---|---|---|---|
| small box | string | sandpaper | tape |
| sand | spring scale | wax paper | |

## PROCEDURE

1. Fill the box half full of sand.
2. Tie a string around the box. Then, hook the spring scale to the string.
3. Pull the scale to move the box. Record the amount of force needed to move the box on the chart.
4. Put the sandpaper on the table. Tape it to the table. Set the box on it. Pull the box across the sandpaper. Record the amount of force needed to move the box on the chart.
5. Put the wax paper on the table. Tape it to the table. Set the box on it. Pull the box across the wax paper. Record the amount of force needed to move the box on the chart.

### SURFACE FRICTION

| Surface | Force |
|---|---|
| Table | |
| Sandpaper | |
| Wax paper | |

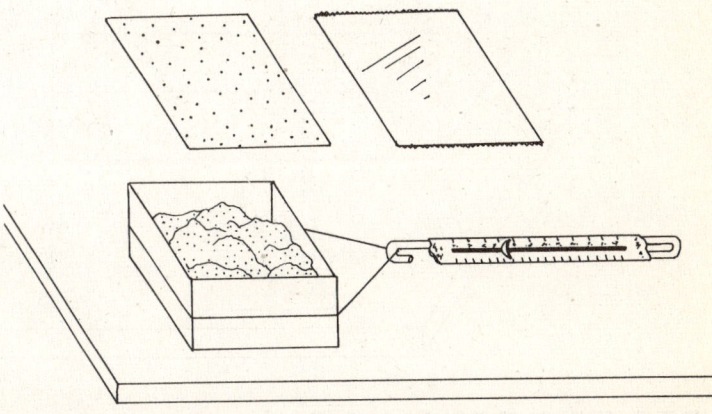

## DRAWING CONCLUSIONS

1. Over which surface was the most force used? Explain.
2. On which surface was the friction the least?
3. How is friction used on a bike?
4. Why do your hands get warm when you rub them together?

Name _____  Date _____

# How Do Wheels Reduce Friction?

Wheels help reduce friction because only a small part of the surface rubs against another object. Do this activity to demonstrate.

**MATERIALS**

| shoe box | string | 3 pencils |
| 4 books | spring scale | 8 marbles |

## PROCEDURE

1. Put all the books in the shoe box.
2. Tie a string around the box. Then, hook the spring scale to the string.
3. Pull the box across the table using the spring scale. Record how much force is needed to pull the box on the chart.
4. Put the pencils under the box. Now pull the scale to pull the box across the table. Record how much force is needed to pull the box on the chart.
5. Put the marbles under the box. Space them so they are equally spread under the box. Now pull the scale to pull the box across the table. Record how much force is needed to pull the box on the chart.

**WHEELS AND FRICTION**

| Surface | Force |
|---------|-------|
| Table   |       |
| Pencils |       |
| Marbles |       |

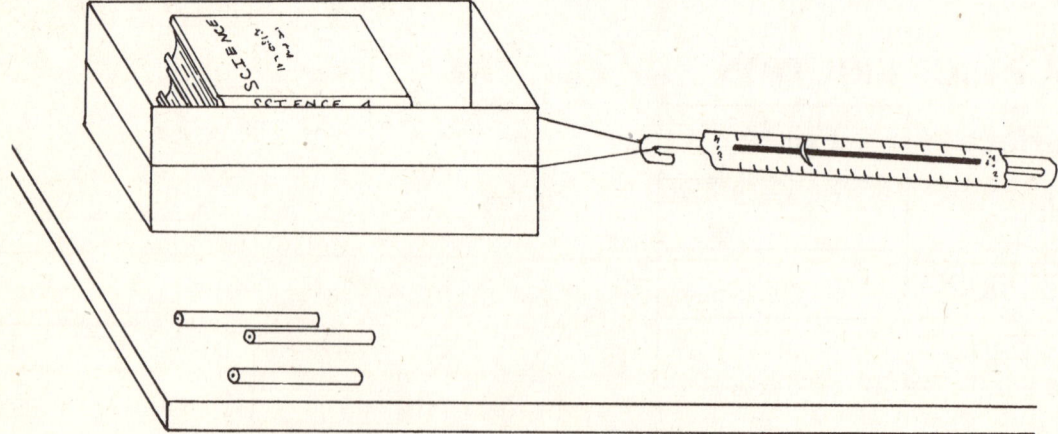

## DRAWING CONCLUSIONS

1. Which of the objects act like wheels? Explain.
2. In which example was friction the greatest? Explain.
3. In which example was friction the least? Explain.
4. List some ways you use wheels every day.

Name _____   Date _____

# Can You Make a Compass?

A compass is a free-floating magnet, called a needle, that turns freely inside a case. A compass works because the Earth is like a giant magnet, with magnetic north and south poles that are located very near the true North and South poles of the Earth. A compass works because the north-seeking pole of the compass needle is attracted to the north magnetic pole of the Earth. In this project, you will make a compass.

### MATERIALS

1 polystyrene foam cup or a piece of cork
scissors
1 bar magnet
1 needle
1 small bowl or flat dish of water

## PROCEDURE

1. Cut a small piece of polystyrene foam about 1 in. (2.5 cm) square. CAUTION: Be careful when handling the scissors.
2. Use one end of the bar magnet to stroke the needle. Do not rub back and forth, but stroke from the middle of the needle toward the point, 10 times.
3. Set the needle on the polystyrene foam or cork and float it in the middle of the dish of water.
4. Be sure the area is clear of any large metal objects that could attract the needle. The table should not contain any metal parts.
5. The point of the needle should point north. If you have a commercial compass, use it to test the accuracy of yours.

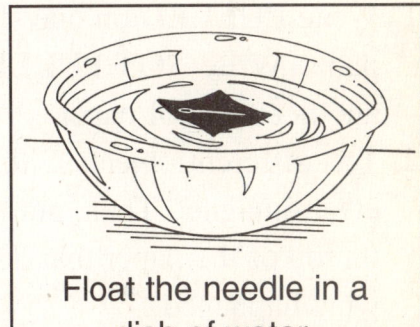
Float the needle in a dish of water.

## DRAWING CONCLUSIONS

1. Why was only one end of the magnet used to stroke the needle?
2. Why would other metal objects in the area affect your results?

**MORE IDEAS**

1. Use the bar magnet you used in the above project and tie a string to the center of it until it is balanced and swings horizontally. Tie the other end of the string to a stationary object so that the magnet is swinging freely. Leave the magnet until it stops moving.
2. What do you predict will happen? Why? Use a compass to see if your bar magnet is also pointing north. (Do not hold the compass close to the magnet.)

www.svschoolsupply.com
© Steck-Vaughn Company

75

Unit 3: Physical Science
Science Projects 3–4, SV 6910-8

Name _____  Date _____

# Do Magnets and Electromagnets Work the Same?

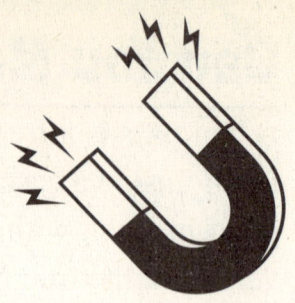

An electromagnet is a magnet made from a wire, a nail, and a dry cell. The current of the dry cell causes the nail to have a magnetic force. Does an electromagnet work as well as a magnet? Try this activity to find out.

**MATERIALS**

electromagnet
paper clips
magnet
stack of paper

objects to test, such as buttons, coins, aluminum foil, rubber band, thumbtack, nail, and pencil

## PROCEDURE

1. Write **PULLED** on one sheet of paper. Write **NOT PULLED** on another sheet of paper.
2. Test different objects with the electromagnet. Then, put each object on top of the paper that describes what happened.
3. Test the objects again. Use the magnet this time. Was there any object that was pulled by the electromagnet but not by the magnet? Was there any object pulled by the magnet but not by the electromagnet?
4. Now, find out which magnet can hold more. Line up some paper clips. See how many paper clips the electromagnet can hold.

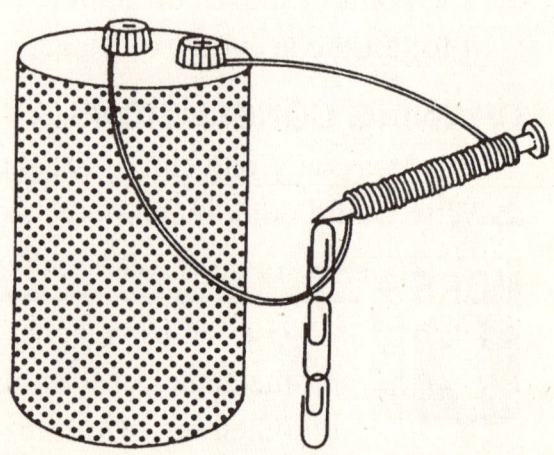

www.svschoolsupply.com
© Steck-Vaughn Company

76

Unit 3: Physical Science
Science Projects 3–4, SV 6910-8

# Do Magnets and Electromagnets Work the Same?, page 2

5. Use the magnet to make a line of paper clips.
6. Place a sheet of paper over a paper clip. Can the electromagnet still pick up the clip? Find the greatest number of sheets of paper it can pull through.
7. Repeat Step 6 using a magnet. Find the greatest number of sheets of paper it can pull through.

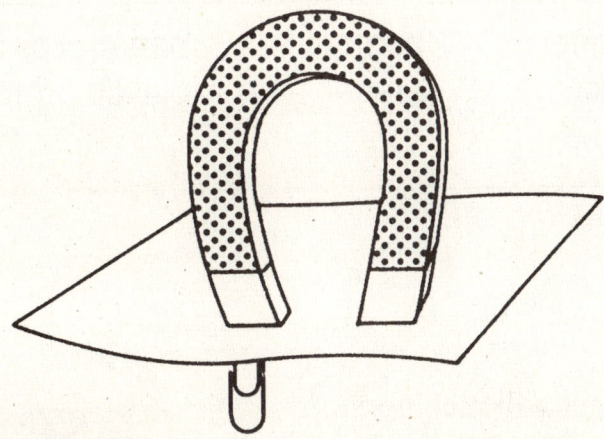

## DRAWING CONCLUSIONS

1. Did the electromagnet or magnet attract more objects?
2. Did the electromagnet or magnet hold more paper clips in a line?
3. Which is stronger, the electromagnet or the magnet?

**MORE IDEAS**

1. Include your setup and result sheets with your display.
2. Do research to find other ways magnets and electromagnets are alike and different. For example, can an electromagnet be turned off?
3. Find out different ways magnets and electromagnets are used in business and industry.
4. Would a magnet or an electromagnet work better in a junkyard?

Name _____ Date _____

# What Can a Magnet Pick Up?

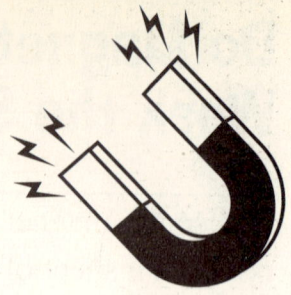

Magnets pick up and stick to many different things. They come in different shapes and sizes. They have different strengths, depending on their size. They have a force called a magnetic force. If not stored properly, magnets can lose their magnetic force. What kinds of things can a magnet pick up? Do this activity to find out.

### MATERIALS

| magnet | penny | paper clips |
| pencil | eraser | plastic protractor or ruler |
| screw | | |

## PROCEDURE

1. Place all the objects except the magnet on a table.
2. Predict what the magnet will pick up. Record your predictions on the chart.
3. Use the magnet to try to pick up each object. Which objects did the magnet pick up? Record your findings on the chart.

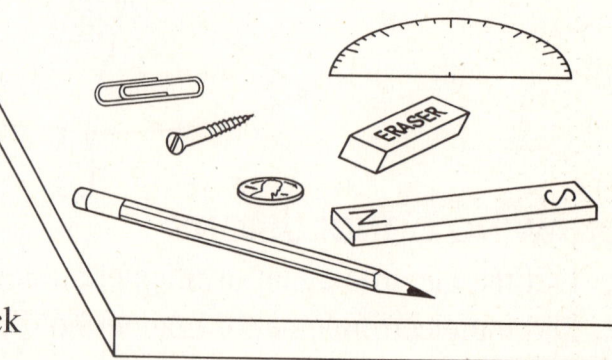

### WHAT MAGNETS PICK UP

| Object | Prediction | Result |
|--------|------------|--------|
|        |            |        |
|        |            |        |
|        |            |        |
|        |            |        |
|        |            |        |
|        |            |        |

## DRAWING CONCLUSIONS

1. Which objects stuck to the magnet?
2. What are these objects made of?
3. Name three other objects that a magnet can pick up.

Name _____  Date _____

# What Is Static Electricity?

Electric charges can be either moving or still. In an electric circuit, the charges move along the wires. If an object is rubbed, it sometimes gains an electric charge, but the charges do not move in the object. They are said to be "static" and the object has "static electricity." An object with static electricity acts like a magnet. Because it has either gained or lost electrons, an object that has static charge either attracts or repels other objects. In this project, you will investigate the effects of static electricity.

**MATERIALS**

2 balloons
string
several of the following: salt, parsley flakes, puffed rice cereal, polystyrene foam broken into tiny pieces

## PROCEDURE

1. Blow up and tie one balloon.
2. Hold the balloon with one hand and rub it against your hair for about 30 strokes. Rub in only one direction.
3. Hold the balloon up to a wall and let go. Observe what happens.
4. Rub the balloon on your hair again and hold it close to a friend's hair. Observe what happens.
5. Sprinkle some salt, parsley flakes, puffed rice cereal, or tiny polystyrene foam pieces on a table.
6. Again stroke your hair with the balloon in one direction about 30 times. Hold it several inches above the small items on the table. Observe what happens.
7. Blow up and tie the other balloon. Tie a piece of string to each balloon.
8. Again stroke your hair with one balloon.
9. Hold both strings attached to the balloons in one hand so that the balloons hang freely. Observe what happens.

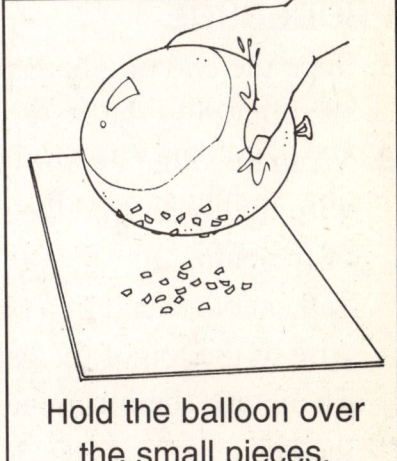

Hold the balloon over the small pieces.

## DRAWING CONCLUSIONS

1. Using the information in the introduction, can you explain which object lost electrons—the hair or the balloon? Give the reason for your answer.
2. Why did the balloon stick to the wall?
3. Why did it pick up small objects?

Name _____ Date _____

# Which Materials Conduct Electricity?

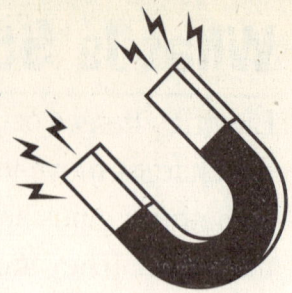

Electric currents can move through some materials more easily than others. Material that a current can move through is called a conductor. Most metals conduct electricity. They are like a wire that a current moves through. Your body is also a good conductor. Every circuit needs a generator, a conductor, and an electrical user. Do this activity to learn more about electricity.

## MATERIALS

3 lengths of wire, each 30 centimeters long
clear tape
D-size battery
toothpick
key
bulb and socket

NOTE: This experiment must be done with an adult.

## PROCEDURE

1. Tape the end of a bare wire to the bottom of the battery.
2. Wrap the other end of the wire tightly around the socket of the bulb.
3. Tape another end of a bare wire to the top of the battery. Then, tape the other end to the key.

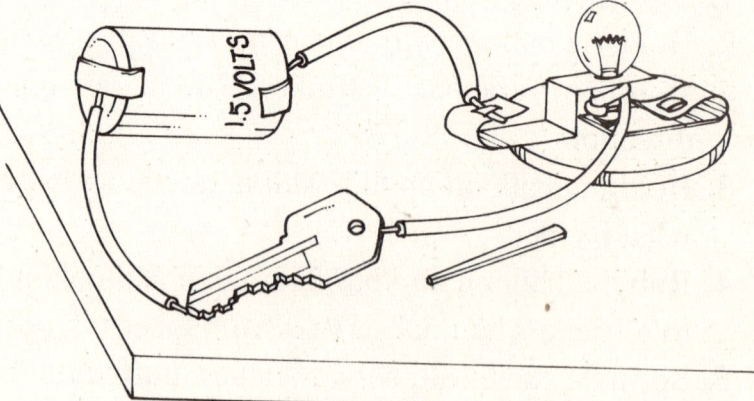

4. Wrap the end of the third wire around the metal part of the bulb.
5. Touch the third wire to the key to make a closed circuit. What happens?
6. Replace the key with a toothpick. Repeat. What happens?

## DRAWING CONCLUSIONS

1. Was the key a conductor?
2. Was the toothpick a conductor?
3. What is needed to make an electric circuit?
4. What kind of material is a good conductor?

Name _____ Date _____

# What Is White Light Made Of?

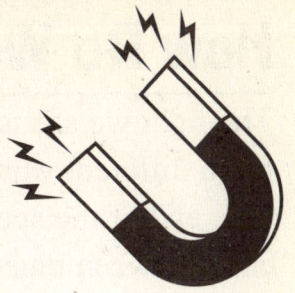

White light is light that comes from a natural source. It is clear and generally not seen. When this kind of light passes through glass or water, it changes speed and bends, producing a spectrum of seven colors. Do this activity to learn about the spectrum.

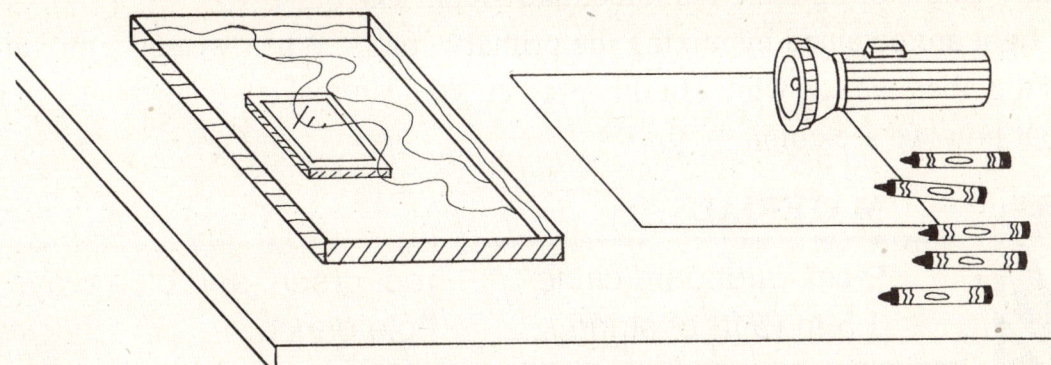

### MATERIALS

- flashlight or sunlight
- mirror
- tape
- white paper
- crayons (red, yellow, blue, green, orange, violet, purple)
- tray of water

## PROCEDURE

1. Place the tray of water near a wall. Set the mirror in the water.
2. Tape a piece of white paper on the wall.
3. Shine the flashlight at the mirror. Move the flashlight around until you can see a reflection on the paper. What colors do you see?
4. Use your crayons to draw the order of the colors on a sheet of paper.

## DRAWING CONCLUSIONS

1. What is the order of the colors in the spectrum?
2. Do you think the order of the spectrum changes? Explain.
3. How did the water help to make the spectrum?
4. How did the mirror help to make the spectrum?

## MORE IDEAS

1. Include your setup with your display. Produce the spectrum for the judges.
2. Do research on prisms and other things that can produce a spectrum.

# How Do We See Colors?

The light we see is made up of a spectrum of colors. Each color has a different wavelength. The shortest wavelengths form the blue end of the spectrum. The longest wavelengths form the red end. Between blue and red are the other colors of the spectrum. The primary colors of light are red, blue, and green. The other colors of light are obtained by mixing the primary colors. When we see a mixture of all colors together, we see white. In this project, you can make a color wheel to learn more about how we see color.

**MATERIALS**

9-cm cardboard circle   red, green, and blue crayons
1.5 m (5 ft) of string   hole punch

## PROCEDURE

1. Divide the circle into three equal sections as shown in the drawing.
2. Using the crayons, color one section red, the second blue, and the third green.

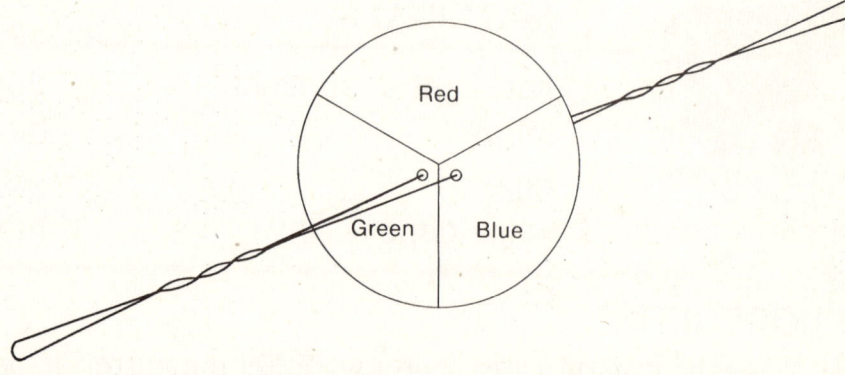

3. Punch two small holes in the wheel about 3 mm (0.1 in.) on each side of the center. See the drawing.
4. Pass the string through two holes as shown. Tie the ends.
5. Turn the wheel to twist the string. You can now spin the wheel by pulling the string in and out. (This may take some practice.)

## DRAWING CONCLUSIONS

1. What happens to the colors as the wheel spins?
2. What color do you see?

**MORE IDEAS**

1. Do research to learn how the rods and cones of the human eye allow us to see colors.
2. Do research to learn how a television uses the three primary colors to produce a full-color picture.

Name _____  Date _____

# Does Light Travel in a Straight Line?

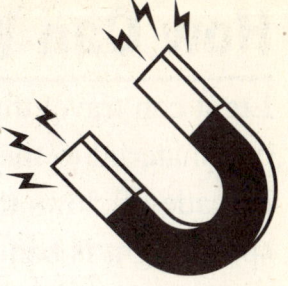

Like sound, light moves out in all directions from its source. It moves very fast. If something blocks the light, the light is reflected back. The blocked object makes a shadow behind. A shadow is a dark place that has the shape of the object. Because of the shadows, we know that light travels in a straight line.

**MATERIALS**
- 3 index cards
- clay
- flashlight
- hole punch
- ruler

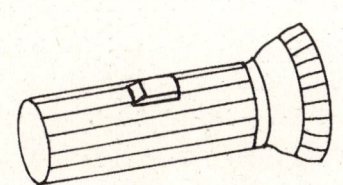 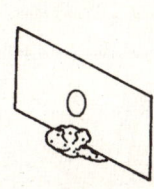  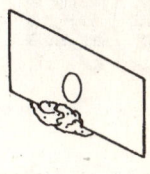

## PROCEDURE

1. With the index cards held together, punch a hole through them. Make sure the hole is in the same spot on each.
2. Place clay balls in a straight line about 5 cm apart from each other.
3. Stick a card in each ball. Try to line up the holes.
4. Shine the light through the holes. Hold your hand open behind the last card.
5. Slide the second card to one side. What do you see?

## DRAWING CONCLUSIONS

1. Did the light travel through the holes when they were lined up?
2. What happened to the light when you moved the middle card?
3. When did you see shadows? Explain.
4. Does light travel in a straight line? How do you know?
5. What happens to light when it is blocked by an object?

# How Can You Bend a Light Beam?

Light can travel through some objects. When light passes from one material to the next, it bends. The kind of material the object is made of slows the speed of light. Because of the change in speed, light is bent. If you have ever seen a straw in a clear cup of water, the straw looks as if it is broken. The speed of light as it passes from air to water changes, making the straw look as if it is cut in half at the water's surface.

**MATERIALS**

- light box or flashlight
- water
- black paper
- clear, plastic shoe box
- milk
- spray bottle

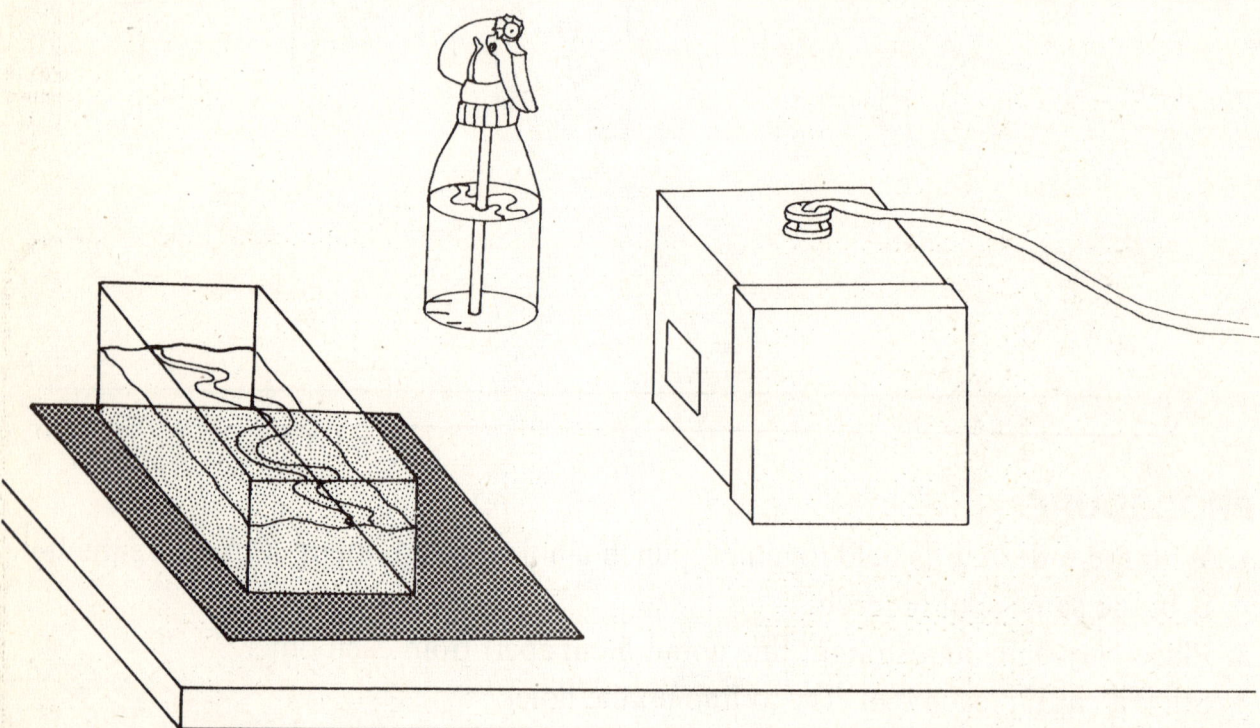

## PROCEDURE

1. Place the shoe box on the black paper. Fill the shoe box with water.
2. Mix 4 or 5 drops of milk in the water.
3. Shine the light through one long side of the shoe box.
4. Spray some water in the beam of light. Look down from above. What do you see?
5. Try to bend the light by moving the flashlight to a new position. What happens now?

Name _____ Date _____

# How Can You Bend a Light Beam?, page 2

**DRAWING CONCLUSIONS**

1. What happens to the light beam when the flashlight points straight to the side of the shoe box?
2. If you change the angle of the flashlight, what happens?
3. What can you change to make the light beam bend even more?
4. Look at the picture of the pencil in the glass. Explain why the pencil looks broken.

 **MORE IDEAS**

1. Do your experiment for the judges. Explain what causes the light to bend.
2. Include other examples of bending light in your display. Put a pencil in a glass of water as shown on this page.
3. Do research on refraction. Refraction deals with the bending of light. How is refraction different from reflection?

Name _____  Date _____

# Does Light Spread Out from Its Source?

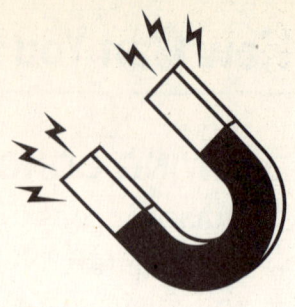

When light is near its source, it is very bright. As it moves out in all directions, it gets dimmer the farther it is from its source. It also spreads out more. Do this activity to demonstrate.

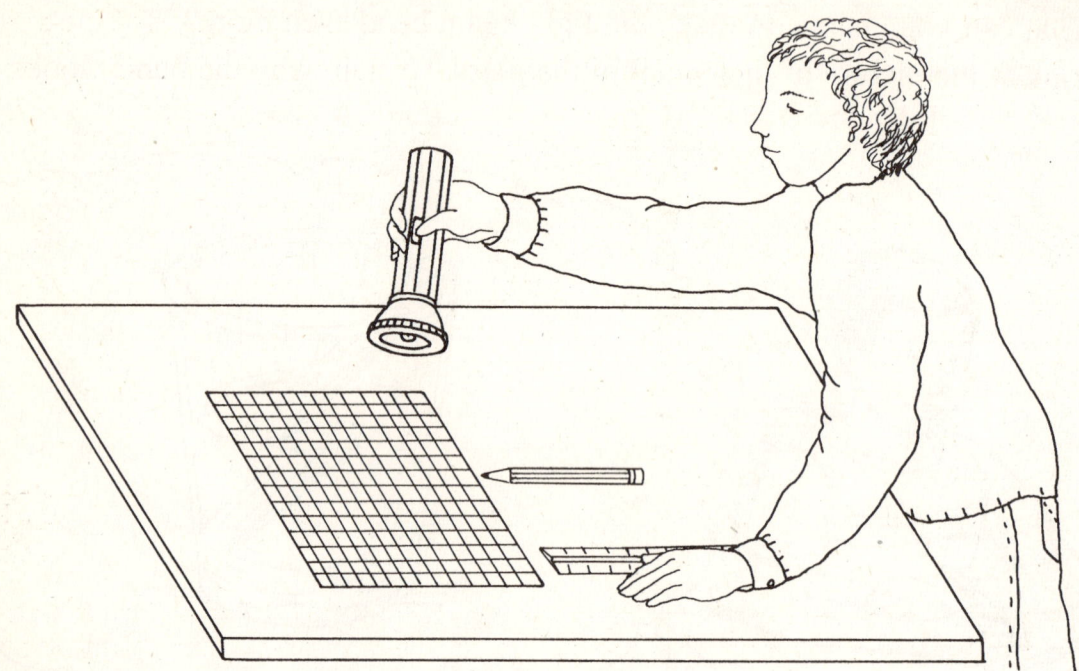

## MATERIALS

ruler           flashlight
pencil        centimeter graph paper

## PROCEDURE

1. Work with a partner. Lay the graph paper flat on a table. Hold the flashlight straight up and down. Hold the ruler beside it. Make sure the flashlight is 2 cm from the paper.
2. Look at the circle of light. Have your partner mark four sides of the circle of light, opposite to each other, on the paper.
3. Raise the flashlight to 4 cm. Repeat Step 2.
4. Continue to raise the flashlight 2 cm at a time and mark the light circles until the light reaches the edge of the paper.
5. Turn off the flashlight. Use the ruler to measure the diameter, the distance from side to side, of each circle.
6. Record the diameter measurements in the chart on the next page.

Name _____  Date _____

# Does Light Spread Out from Its Source?, page 2

## DRAWING CONCLUSIONS
1. What happened to the circle of light as you moved the flashlight away from the paper?
2. What happened to the brightness of the light?
3. What two things happen to light as it gets farther from its source?

## MEASUREMENT OF LIGHT

| Distance to Paper | Diameter of Light Circle |
|---|---|
| 2 cm | |
| 4 cm | |
| 6 cm | |
| 8 cm | |
| 10 cm | |

**MORE IDEAS**
1. Include your results chart with your display. Do the activity for the judges.
2. Do research on laser light. Does laser light act like regular light? Does laser light spread out from its source?

www.svschoolsupply.com
© Steck-Vaughn Company

87

Unit 3: Physical Science
Science Projects 3–4, SV 6910-8

Name _____  Date _____

# What Makes a Good Reflector?

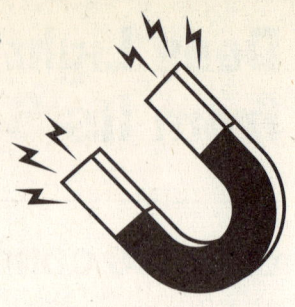

Good reflectors usually have shiny, smooth surfaces. They must be shiny so that the light will bounce back. They must be smooth so that the light will stay together and not scatter. You will not be able to see the beam as clearly when it scatters. Do this activity to learn the qualities of a good reflector.

| MATERIALS | | |
|---|---|---|
| flashlight | mirror | 2 squares of foil |

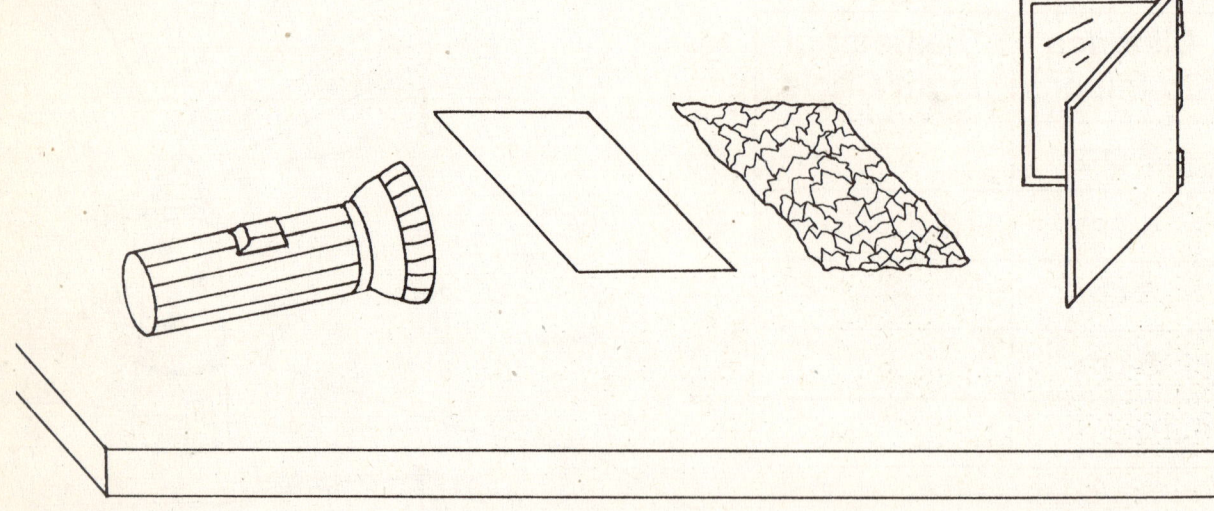

## PROCEDURE

1. Crumple one sheet of foil so the surface is uneven. Then, flatten it out.
2. Hold the mirror in one hand and the flashlight in the other. Stand next to a wall. Aim the light on the mirror so that a reflection shines on the wall. What do you see?
3. Repeat Step 2 using the smooth foil. How does it compare to the reflection you saw using the mirror?
4. Repeat Step 2 using the crumpled foil. How does it compare to the reflections you saw using the mirror and smooth foil?

## DRAWING CONCLUSIONS

1. Which material reflected the beam of light best? Explain.
2. Which material reflected the beam of light the least? Explain.
3. Which material makes the best reflector? Why?
4. Which piece of foil reflected better? Why?
5. What other materials would make good reflectors?

Name _____   Date _____

# Does Sound Travel Through All Solids the Same?

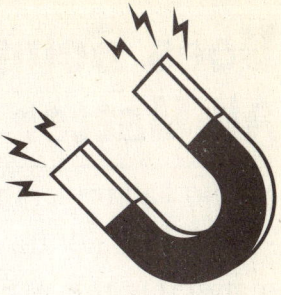

Sound can travel through a solid object. Does it travel better through some solids than others? Does it travel better through soft materials than hard ones? Do this activity to find out.

**MATERIALS**

pencil    sponge    wooden ruler    metal pot

## PROCEDURE

1. Work with a partner. Press your ear to the surface of a table. Cover your other ear with your hand.
2. Your partner should stand at least one meter from you. Have your partner hold a wooden ruler upright on the table, as shown. Your partner should gently tap the top of the ruler with a pencil.
3. Then, have your partner hold the sponge on the table. Your partner should tap on the sponge with a pencil. Is the sound louder, softer, or the same as when the ruler was tapped?
4. Next, have your partner tap the metal pot with a pencil. Is the sound louder, softer, or the same as when the ruler was tapped?

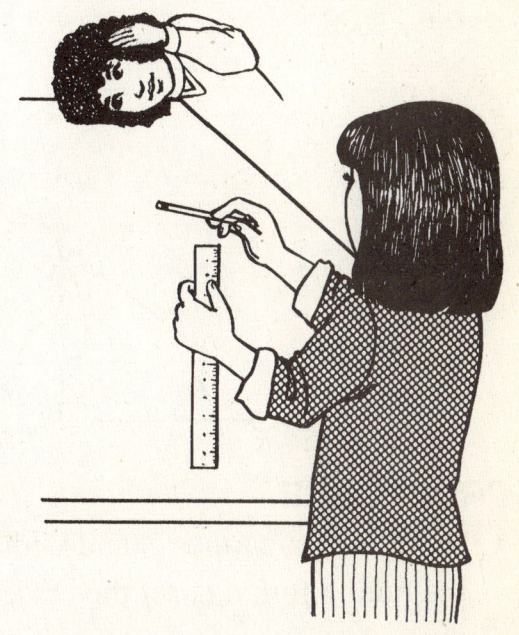

## DRAWING CONCLUSIONS

1. Which tapped object was the loudest?
2. Does sound travel better through some solids than others? Explain.
3. Does sound travel better through soft objects or hard objects?

**MORE IDEAS**

1. Include your setup and your results sheet with your display.
2. Do research on soundproofing. What kinds of materials are used to soundproof rooms?

# Does Sound Travel Through All Matter the Same?

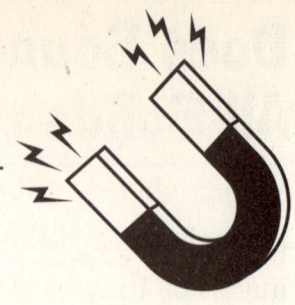

Sound can travel through solids, liquids, and gases. However, sound does not travel at the same speed through each kind of matter. Do this activity to learn the differences.

**MATERIALS**

ruler  
rubber eraser  
tuning fork  
water-filled balloon

## PROCEDURE

1. Work with a partner. Stand with your back to your partner. Have the partner strike the tuning fork against the eraser and hold it about 10 cm from your ear. Listen for the sound.
2. Switch places. Repeat Step 1 so that your partner can listen to the sound of the tuning fork.
3. Put your ear against the table. Have your partner strike the tuning fork against the eraser and hold the handle about 20 cm from your head. Listen to the sound. Switch places and repeat.
4. Place the water-filled balloon on the edge of the table. Have your partner strike the tuning fork against the eraser and hold the handle gently to the balloon. (Be careful not to break the balloon with the tuning fork.) Listen for the sound.

## DRAWING CONCLUSIONS

1. Did sound travel better through a solid, liquid, or gas? Explain.
2. Through which matter did the sound not move as well? Explain.

# Does Sound Travel Through All Matter the Same?, page 2

**MORE IDEAS**

1. Include your setup with your display. Do the activity for the judges.
2. As you have found, sound travels faster through some materials than others. Read the chart below. It shows how fast sound travels through some common materials in one second. Include the chart with your display.

### SPEED OF SOUND

| Material | Distance Sound Travels in 1 Second |
|---|---|
| Water | 1,433 meters |
| Steel | 4,999 meters |
| Granite | 6,096 meters |
| Cork | 503 meters |
| Brick | 3,627 meters |
| Lead | 1,219 meters |
| Iron | 4,877 meters |
| Space | 0 meters |
| Air (at 0° C) | 332 meters |

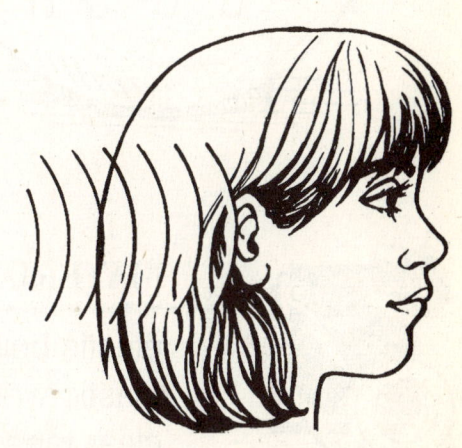

## MORE CONCLUSIONS

1. Does sound travel through space?
2. Of the materials listed, through which does sound move the slowest?
3. Of the materials listed, through which does sound travel the fastest?

# How Do Sounds Vibrate?

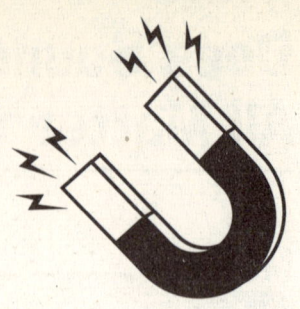

Sound travels in waves. As the waves move out and away from the place where the sound starts, they push against other objects in their path. As the sound wave hits an object, it causes the object to vibrate. The louder the sound, the harder the sound wave hits and the more the object vibrates.

### MATERIALS

| | |
|---|---|
| plastic bowl | metal pot |
| plastic wrap | wooden spoon |
| clear tape | meter stick |
| uncooked rice | |

## PROCEDURE

1. Stretch the plastic wrap across the top of the plastic bowl. Tape the wrap in place, making sure the wrap is pulled as tightly as it can be.
2. Place the bowl on the table. Place about 20 grains of rice on the plastic so they do not touch.
3. Hold the metal pot near the bowl. Hit the pot with the spoon gently. Then, hit the pot hard. Watch the rice carefully each time. What happens?
4. Hold the pot about one meter from the bowl. Gently tap the pot with the spoon. What happens to the rice this time?
5. Remove the rice. Hold the pot near the bowl again. Rest your fingers lightly on the plastic wrap. Have a classmate gently hit the pot. Then, have your classmate hit the pot harder. Do you feel a difference in the movement of the plastic wrap?

# How Do Sounds Vibrate?, page 2

**DRAWING CONCLUSIONS**

1. What made the rice move?
2. What happened when the pot was hit gently?
3. What happened when the pot was hit hard?
4. How close must the pot be to the bowl to make the wrap move?
5. How can sounds make objects move?
6. How is the plastic wrap on the bowl like your eardrum?

**MORE IDEAS**

1. As you may recall, your ear is almost like a megaphone that helps you hear sounds better. As sounds hit your outer ear, they are passed into the inner ear. There they hit the eardrum, which vibrates and sends signals to the brain. Those signals are read by the brain as sounds.
2. You can make an eardrum model by stretching plastic wrap over a bowl. Put rice or sugar on the plastic wrap.
3. Strike a metal pot hard with a spoon. Does the rice or sugar vibrate? Is this like a shout or a whisper?
4. Strike a metal pot softly with a spoon. Does the rice or sugar vibrate? Is this like a shout or a whisper?

Name _____  Date _____

# What Causes Sound to Change?

Sound is made when objects vibrate. The size of the object or the material the object is made of can affect the sound it makes. By changing either the size or the material, you can change the sound.

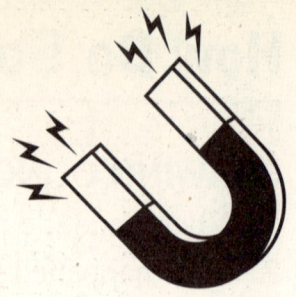

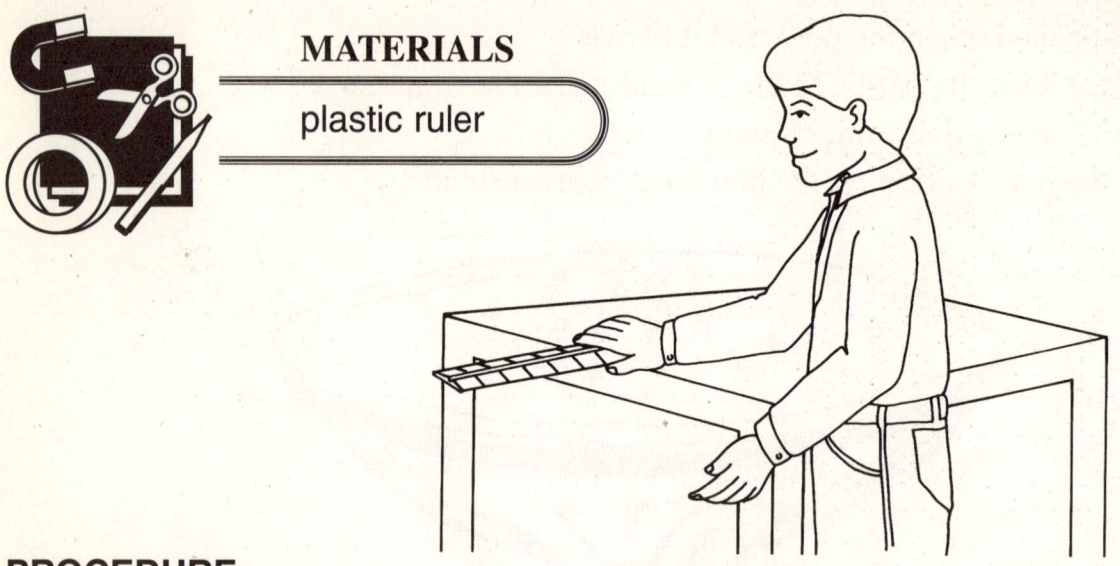

**MATERIALS**

plastic ruler

## PROCEDURE

1. Place the ruler on the edge of a table so that half of it hangs off.
2. Hold the end of the ruler flat against the table with one hand. With the other hand, lightly snap the end of the ruler that hangs off the table. Listen to the sound.
3. Push the ruler back, so that less of the ruler hangs off the table. What do you think will happen to the sound now? Repeat Step 2. Record your observations in the chart.
4. Push the ruler so that most of it hangs off the table. What do you think will happen to the sound now? Repeat Step 2. Record your observations in the chart.

### RULER SOUNDS

| Length | How Sound Changed |
|---|---|
| Shorter | |
| Longer | |

## DRAWING CONCLUSIONS

1. What happened when you hit the free end of the ruler in Step 2?
2. What happened to the sound when the ruler stopped?
3. How did the sound change when the ruler was made shorter?
4. What happened when the ruler was made longer?
5. What causes sound to change?

Name _____  Date _____

# How Can You Change the Pitch of a Sound?

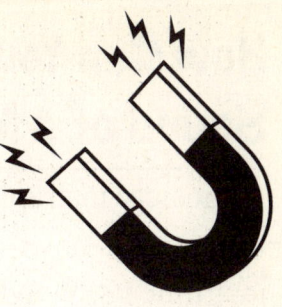

Pitch is the highness or lowness of a sound. The pitch depends on vibrations. More vibrations mean a higher pitch. A flute has a high pitch, and a bass violin has a low pitch.

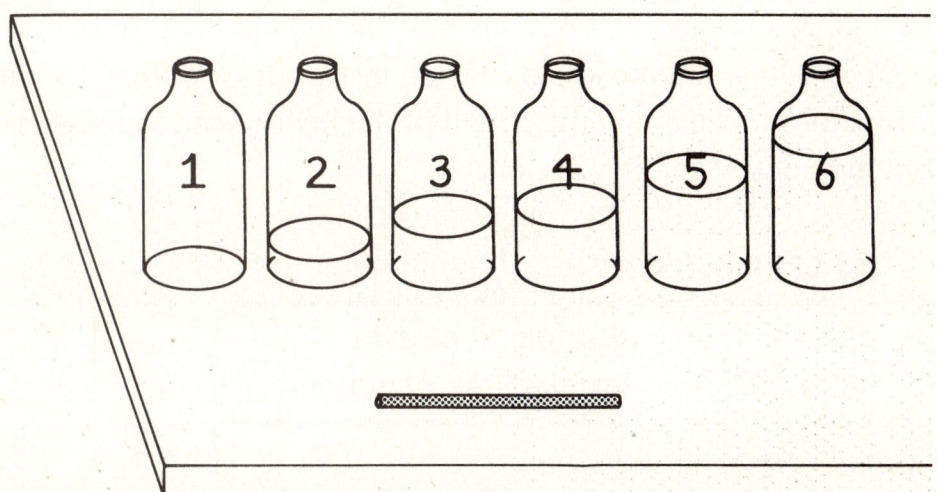

**MATERIALS**

| water | 6 glass bottles of the same size |
| wooden stick | permanent marker |

## PROCEDURE

1. Line up the bottles in a straight row.
2. Number them 1 through 6 with the permanent marker.
3. Leave the first bottle empty. Pour a small amount of water into bottle 2. Gradually increase the amount of water in the bottles. Fill bottle 6 so that it is almost full.
4. Tap each bottle with the wooden stick. What happens to each bottle? Do you hear different pitches?

## DRAWING CONCLUSIONS

1. Which bottle has the shortest air column?
2. Which bottle has the longest air column?
3. Which bottle produced the highest pitch?
4. Which bottle produced the lowest pitch?
5. What is the relationship between the amount of air in a bottle and the pitch of the sound it makes when it is tapped?

Name _____  Date _____

# How Can You Change the Sound of a Musical Instrument?

A musical instrument makes vibrations at the same rate. String instruments have strings that vibrate. There are two kinds of wind instruments: woodwinds and brass. A woodwind is made of wood. A brass instrument is made of metal. Woodwinds make sounds when air moves across a reed, a thin piece of wood. In brass instruments, sound is made by the vibrations of the player's lips. In both kinds of wind instruments, different sounds are made as the vibrations travel along the length of the instrument. Percussion instruments make vibrations when they are hit.

**MATERIALS**

ruler  4 drinking straws
scissors  small glass of water

## PROCEDURE

1. Make musical instruments out of the straws. Flatten about 3 cm of one end of a straw. Rub the scissors over the edges to make them flat.
2. Cut the corners off each flattened side of the straw. This will serve as the reed of a wind instrument.

3. Dip a finger in the water. Lightly rub your finger over the "reed" of the straw.
4. Blow into the reed. What did you hear?
5. Cut the remaining straws into different lengths. Repeat Steps 1 through 3 to make more wind instruments. Predict how you think the length of each straw will affect how it sounds. Try each one.

## DRAWING CONCLUSIONS

1. What caused the sounds?
2. How were the sounds of the longer instruments different from the sounds of the shorter instruments?
3. How are your instruments like woodwind instruments?
4. What caused the sound when you blew through the straw?
5. How did the sounds of the different instruments compare with your predictions?

# Science Projects, Grades 3–4

## Table of Contents

Introduction .................................2
FOSS Correlation ............................3
Types of Projects ...........................4
Science Fair Checklist ......................6
The Scientific Method ......................7
Your Science Fair Project ..................8
Science Fair Notebook ......................9
Presenting the Project ....................10

### Unit 1: Earth Science
Sample Earth Science Project ..............11
How Hard Is a Rock? .......................12
How Are Rocks Broken Down? ................14
How Does a Volcano Erupt? .................15
What Does Erosion Do? .....................16
How Can Erosion Be Slowed? ................17
What Is Soil Made Of? .....................18
Where Can You Find Air Pollution? .........19
What Will Rust? ...........................20
Can You Take Water Out of the Air? ........21
How Long Does Water Take to Evaporate? ....22
Can You Record Changes in Humidity? .......24
How Can You Measure Humidity? .............26
Can Fresh Water Be Made from Salt Water? ..28
Is Your Water Hard or Soft? ...............29
How Strong Is Surface Tension? ............30
Do Different Liquids Have Different Freezing Points? 31
Can the Freezing Point of Water Be Lowered? ..32
Which Heats Faster, Soil or Water? ........33
How Can You Trap the Sun's Energy? ........34
Is It Cooler Underground or Aboveground? ..36
Can You Make a Cloud? .....................37
What Does the Solar System Look Like? .....38
How Much Would You Weigh on Other Planets? .39
Is the Earth Really Moving? ...............40

### Unit 2: Life Science
Sample Life Science Project ...............41
How Do Plants Get Water? ..................42
How Much Water Is in Fruits and Vegetables? .43
Can You Grow Plants Without Seeds? ........44
Can You Grow Plants Without Soil? .........46
Can You Grow a Kitchen Garden? ............48

Do Plants Need Light? .....................49
Do Plants Move? ...........................50
How Do Plants Protect Soil? ...............51
Can You Make Paper? .......................52
What Foods Do Insects Like? ...............54
How Does Color Protect Animals? ...........55
How Do Animals Survive in the Cold? .......56
How Does a Caterpillar Metamorphose? ......58
How Can You Keep Cool on a Hot Day? .......59
How Do Your Heart and Lungs Work? .........60
How Does Activity Affect a Person's Pulse Rate? ..62
How Are Reflexes Related to Reaction Time? ..63
What Is an Optical Illusion? ..............64
Can You Find Fat in Foods? ................65
What Happens to Dead Organisms? ...........66

### Unit 3: Physical Science
Sample Physical Science Project ...........67
Do Inclined Planes Make Work Easier? ......68
How Does a Lever Make Work Easier? ........70
How Do a Wheel and Axle Make Work Easier? ..71
How Do Pulleys Make Work Easier? ..........72
How Is Friction Affected by Different Surfaces? ..73
How Do Wheels Reduce Friction? ............74
Can You Make a Compass? ...................75
Do Magnets and Electromagnets Work the Same? ..76
What Can a Magnet Pick Up? ................78
What Is Static Electricity? ...............79
Which Materials Conduct Electricity? ......80
What Is White Light Made Of? ..............81
How Do We See Colors? .....................82
Does Light Travel in a Straight Line? .....83
How Can You Bend a Light Beam? ............84
Does Light Spread Out from Its Source? ....86
What Makes a Good Reflector? ..............88
Does Sound Travel Through All Solids the Same? ..89
Does Sound Travel Through All Matter the Same? ..90
How Do Sounds Vibrate? ....................92
What Causes Sound to Change? ..............94
How Can You Change the Pitch of a Sound? ..95
How Can You Change the Sound
   of a Musical Instrument? ..............96

# Introduction

We arise in a new world every day. Our lives are caught in a whirlwind of change. New wonders are discovered on a daily basis. Technology is carrying us rapidly into the 21st century. How will our children keep pace with this constant change? We must provide them with the tools necessary to journey confidently into the future. Those tools can be found in a sound science education. One guidepost to a good foundation in science is the Full Option Science System™ (FOSS) Standards. This book adheres to these standards.

Young students are interested in almost everything around them—the Earth and sky, plants and animals, and the way things work. They should be encouraged to observe their world, the things in it, and their neighbors in the sky. They should take note of the properties of the Earth and its inhabitants and then try to develop their own explanation of why things are the way they are. A basic understanding of science boosts students' understanding of the world around them.

But knowledge without application would be wasted effort. Students should be encouraged to participate in their school science fair. To help facilitate this, *Science Projects* is packed with a variety of projects that students can do easily.

## Organization

*Science Projects* is a handy companion to the regular science curriculum. It is divided into three units: Earth Science; Life Science; and Physical Science. Each unit contains a variety of science projects to spark the interest of science students and to reinforce students' knowledge and understanding of basic principles of science and the world around them.

The introductory section of the book contains several handy forms, charts, and schedules that will help a student to organize and conduct a project more efficiently. The introductory section also contains a correlation of the projects to the FOSS standards.

## Developing a Project

An understanding of science is best promoted by hands-on experience. It is essential that students be given sufficient concrete examples of scientific concepts. Appropriate manipulatives can be bought or made from common everyday objects. Most of the projects can be completed with materials easily accessible to the students.

To help students develop a viable project, consider these guidelines:

1. Decide whether to do individual or group projects.
2. Help students choose a topic that interests them and that is manageable. Make sure a project is appropriate for a student's grade level and ability. Otherwise, that student might become frustrated. This does not mean that you should discourage a student's scientific curiosity. However, some projects are just not appropriate.
3. Encourage students to develop questions and to talk about their questions in class.
4. Help students to decide on one question or problem.
5. Help students to design a logical process for developing the project. Stress that the acquisition of materials is an important part of the project. Some projects also require strict schedules, so students must be willing and able to carry through with the process.
6. Remind students that the Scientific Method will help them to organize their thoughts and activities. Students should keep track of their resources used, whether they are people or print materials. Encourage students to use the Internet to do research on their project.
7. Be sure that you are familiar with the school's science-fair guidelines. Some schools, for example, do not allow glass or any electrical or flammable projects. An exhibit also is usually restricted to three or four feet of table space.

## Judging

Inform the students that a science project is usually judged using three criteria:

1. Exhibition Construction and Display: Creativity, neatness, organization, visual appeal, workmanship, and clarity.
2. Exhibit Notebook: Thoroughness, scientific thought, investigative skills, organization and presentation of data, resources.
3. Knowledge of Topic: Accuracy and completeness of information, clarity of data and results, understanding of topic, oral presentation.